Poh's Kitchen

Poh's Kitchen

My cooking adventures

Poh Ling Yeow

ABC
Books

This book is dedicated firstly to the two most important women in my life, Mum, Christina Yeow and my amazing Great Aunt (Koo Poh), Kim Thoo – for being wonderful examples and igniting my passion in food.

Huge thanks to Dad, Steven, my brother, Casper and wife, Teena, for your support through a year of incredible challenge and change. Thank you to my beautiful Joffy for your saintly patience and unconditional love. To little man, Zed: you are a ray of sunshine in every second of my day. To Matt for your friendship and Sarah for always inspiring me to live a simple, creative life and keep the magic of 'little world', alive!

To my extended family and friends – sorry for being positively absent for the past 12 months. To HarperCollins for helping me fulfil my dream of publishing a cookbook – I still can't believe it's happened. In particular huge thanks to Jo Mackay, Julia Collingwood, Jane Waterhouse and Helen Biles. I'm positive all of you have had evil thoughts of throttling me – I know I haven't been easy to work with, but thank you, thank you for being absolute troopers!

To my second family, the *Poh's Kitchen* team at ABC TV. I have huge admiration for all of you professionally and as people, and thank you for making me look somewhat respectable as a presenter! Special thanks to Margot Phillipson, my TV mum, for coaching me through my neurosis on a daily basis. To Elle, big hugs and 'MEAT!' You are the third arm that I wish I had – you are a superwoman. To Lisa – 'S Knobs!' for understanding the value of having at least one crazy on the books; and Caitlin, I swear I will have some form of a diary next year.

To my gallery directors – Sam and Margot, Libby and Katie – thank you for your support and patience.

And finally to the Australian public for all your well wishes and encouragement, and in particular to South Australians.

contents

introduction

For me cooking is absolutely like painting. It's very much about escaping into a zone that totally consumes and inspires me. Almost every day, someone approaches me to say, 'Poh, I love what you do on TV but I don't cook', which I find completely surprising – every time. I DO understand the notion of watching cooking shows for pure entertainment because I do it too, sometimes even the bad ones (I confess), but don't you want to know the immeasurable joy of dishing up a meal that makes the dinner conversation come to a standstill, your guests' shoulders sag and their eyes shut blissfully as they savour something of your creation? It's brilliant ego fertiliser and the gratification, I tell you, is completely addictive. This and growing up with a mum and Koo Poh or great aunt (who's made a career of shoving mountainous plates of food in front of me with the instruction – 'eat it all!') are what has turned me into a certified feeder.

If you are afraid of failure, you should be more afraid of eating bad food for the rest of your life! It's very empowering to be able to rescue a few sad vegetables from the bottom of the veggie drawer and transform them into a respectable meal. This book is very much for those of you who think you can't cook. You should have seen me in my early 20s, a newlywed dishing up soggy stir-fries, overcooked steak with three veg and powdered mushroom soup poured over the top as the pièce de résistance! So please try. I'll talk you through every step as though you are an alien to all things food. I will share with you everything I know.

I have my demons too. It's strange how differently wired we are when it comes to soaking up things that come easily to us, and yet be a complete sieve with information we find difficult to absorb. For instance, baking is for me like exercise is for those freaks (I say freak from pure envy and admiration) who love to work-out. If I don't bake something at least every second day, I feel a little out of sorts, and yet someone can explain and show me cuts of meat until the cows come home and quite quickly this witless sort of expression takes over my face. It's not that I'm not interested, but I've never been good at cooking big slabs of meat, nor did I grow up with it coming from a Chinese–Malaysian background. For instance, cooking a roast seems quite insurmountable. I do love a good meat and three veg meal, it was the height of western exoticism for me when I first came to Australia, aged 9, and it still holds major novelty value for me as a dinner guest. About 10 Christmases ago, I roasted 2 chooks (served at 10 minutes to midnight, so it was almost Boxing Day breakfast instead), which didn't draw too many compliments, and I haven't revisited the roast since. But for this book, I've finally decided to be brave, so maybe we can imagine holding each others' hands through the roast recipe. Aaaargh, I'm genuinely scared.

You've probably noticed that I'm not a great example of someone who gets it right all the time. For every successful dish I cook, I'm certain every third one is either quite average or disastrous. The trick is to have a thick skin and dogged persistence. Very recently, I ruined one of my favourite pots steaming corn on the cob for my dog! I started a project in another room and forgot to check the water. Before I knew it, I had an incinerated pot with corn perfectly charcoaled on one side. So forgive yourself when you make mistakes and have a bit of chuckle. (And yes, Zed's eyes go as wide as saucers when he spots corn. I can't remember exactly how I discovered this but when he was still a puppy I also trained him how to sit with single thawed frozen peas as the reward. Go figure!) There's absolutely no shame in having a red hot go because let's face it, a recipe that hasn't gone right is usually still edible, so it is useful to be surrounded by a band of healthy and KIND eaters, which brings me to my next tale of cataclysm.

Being very disorganised, I once disappeared into the kitchen during a dinner I was hosting, to make a pear tart dessert. I was gone for a good hour, and in the final flourish of inverting the tart onto another tray for its final bake, the tart somehow became fuel injected and propelled itself with alarming speed towards a corner of the kitchen floor. As it sat there bent over and pathetic, I observed the baking paper had clung faithfully to the tart and I remained optimistic. So I marched into the lounge and explained what had happened and how the tart had unexpectedly sprouted wings. Amazingly, one friend piped up asking 'Is the pie sitting nude on the floor or is the paper still attached? I mean, is there dog hair stuck to it?' I replied with an adamant 'NO!'. I returned the pie to the oven, and although not quite its former self when it re-emerged, everyone scoffed down my dessert without batting an eyelid. So that is the tale of how I shamelessly served up floor pie!

Of course it seemed an impossible task to compile the recipes for this book, even though I had fantasised about writing a cook book for as long as I could remember. There are just so many fantastic recipes I wanted to include, how would I choose? In the end I decided to go with the ones I'm most attached to and make often – all the ones scribbled in my many dog-eared exercise books. More often than not, they are recipes taken from friends that I've added my own twist to. This book definitely does not contain any ground-breaking recipes, but

what I really wanted to do was share recipes with you that will open up your repertoire, expose you to as many processes as possible, so your confidence and skills as a cook, multiply quickly.

At the beginning I was really nervous. As the book seemed to meander wildly between different cultures and styles of cooking, and I began to doubt myself – what is this book about? The only thin connecting thread I could think of was, it's simply stuff I love to cook. Mmmmm, not good enough, I thought, so I perused my quite comprehensive collection of cookbooks, some of which I find utterly beautiful as objects that I love to hold and own but have never cooked from. Then I realised the books I cook from most tend to leap rambunctiously around the world from French pastries to Asian-style soupy noodles and are the ones which have successfully encouraged me to have an open mind and palate. If nothing, this book truly reflects the complete lack of discipline which my friends and family know so well to be me. When I'm working professionally, I know better, but at home, I am horrible at cooking dinners with any sense of cohesion because I'm always trying out new things. So nearly all my dinners are premised with something ridiculous like, 'Okay, tonight we are going to go East Turkestan, Italy and then Malaysia – hope you don't mind?' ... not that I care, but I have to save face just in case someone thinks I actually think I'm dishing up a seamless repertoire!

Earlier, I mentioned multiplying your cooking skills quickly. By this I mean, think and be clever and make the most of any one method or recipe you have learned. This is why I've tried to give you a few variations on one recipe where possible. There's also a fair bit of cross-referencing in the book, so you can get a sense of what goes with what, and get to understand stuff like flavour profiles. I want to get you thinking independently about what you're doing, so you can start to experiment and create your own dishes, not just follow a recipe with your blinkers on.

Also, patience is a virtue, my friend. Most dishes are works in progress, everyone interprets instructions differently and a lot of recipe writing assumes some basic knowledge. Most recipes require cooking a number of times before they are perfected, as there are many variables like the temperature of domestic ovens not being accurate or ingredients not performing optimally because of varying brands and quality. A raw ingredient can sometimes do strange things to a recipe. If, say, the amount of orange juice required in a recipe is 'the juice of one orange' and the orange you're using is small and not very juicy, this may alter the result of the recipe greatly. Another variable is that taste, like many things, is subjective. What may seem to be perfectly seasoned to one person, will be tasteless to another. Consequently, we are always tweaking things to customise recipes to our own liking. I have, however, been mindful of the sensitivity of a tentative cook and have designed the recipes, not always to be simple, but as fail-safe as possible. So please be brave, always try a new recipe with an open mind, but maybe not on the night you're trying to impress someone you've got the hots for.

Don't send yourself into a tailspin trying to cook an impressive feast every night. I for one am quite happy cooking a couple of adventurous meals a week and then diving into a bowl of steam veg with a dollop of butter the rest of the week. I am slavishly addicted to baking frequently though. It's just so nice to have something a bit cheeky to have with coffee in the morning or tea in the afternoon if a friend drops by. Personally, I've come to realise that in the long run, it's much healthier to be a bit naughty and happy, rather than to be 'good' and miserable, not to mention those horrible lapses where you find yourself tucking into a dirty burger with all the trimmings and then a chaser of chips, lollies and chocolate, all in the one sitting. Aaaargh, the self-loathing that follows … you should've just eaten that small slice of banana caramel pie the night before!

Do keep in mind that cooking is a creative process. It's largely about finding interesting ways to solve problems in order to create the desired result. You never stop learning. Even recipes you've cooked for years can continue to evolve and that's what's so incredibly exciting about the world of food – recipes have a life of their own. I always aspire to put my own spin on things and once you've mastered a dish, challenge yourself, refine it with a new technique you've learnt or (my favourite) an unorthodox one you've invented. This is how you become a good cook. Tonight, make something ambitious rather than effortless. Don't let the naysayers intimidate you with cries of 'impossible soufflés' or 'never-rising sponge cakes'. Discover for yourself, be brave and wield your whisk like a warrior!

Lots of love, laughter and a generous sprinkling of luck

Poh x

conversion chart

1 teaspoon = 5ml

1 Australian tablespoon = 20ml (4 teaspoons)

1 UK tablespoon = 15ml (3 teaspoons/½ fl oz)

1 cup = 250ml (8 fl oz)

cup measures

1 cup almond meal	100g	3½ oz
1 cup sugar, brown	185g	6½ oz
1 cup sugar, white	200g	7¾ oz
1 cup caster (superfine) sugar	230g	8 oz
1 cup icing (confectioner's) sugar	125g	4⅓ oz
1 cup plain (all-purpose) flour	125g	4⅓ oz
1 cup long grain white uncooked rice	200g	7¼ oz

liquid conversions

cups	metric	imperial
⅛ cup	30ml	1 fl oz
¼ cup	60ml	2 fl oz
⅓ cup	80ml	2½ fl oz
½ cup	125ml	4 fl oz
¾ cup	185ml	6 fl oz
1 cup	250ml	8 fl oz
1½ cups	375ml	12 fl oz
2 cups	500ml	16 fl oz
4 cups	1 litre	32 fl oz

NOTE that many ingredients, cooking terms and equipment are explained in a glossary at the end of the book.

breakfast

sinful scrambled eggs with sourdough toast

Trimmings

1 sourdough loaf

olive oil

2 brown field mushrooms

1 teaspoon picked thyme leaves

5 tablespoons grated parmesan
  cheese

2 smallish tomatoes

1 clove garlic, peeled

160g baby spinach leaves

chopped flat leaf parsley for garnish

Eggs

6 large free-range eggs

½ cup (125ml) pouring cream

1 tablespoon good quality butter

shaved or grated parmesan cheese,
  to serve

Every time I make this, and it's probably a lot more often than I should, I do feel like I'm going straight to hell. BUT, may I tell you, the cream does magic things and turns the humble googie into folds of delicious, eggy, satin. For the rest of the 'trimmings' I'm behaving – thin sourdough crisps for scooping rather than a lumbering piece of toast and strictly olive oil only to do the veggies in. My favourite way to have scrambled eggs is with nothing but a drizzle of truffle oil and a flat white … Bliss!

serves 2

TRIMMINGS

Using a sharp chef's knife rather than a serrated knife, slice off 4 very thin slices of the sourdough loaf, about 5mm, on the diagonal. Place the slices on a baking tray and drizzle with the olive oil. Grill until golden and very crispy. Set aside.

Slice the mushrooms into 5mm slices. As the slices fall on a slant, like a domino effect, scoop the whole mushroom, keeping the shape, onto a baking tray lined with foil. Drizzle some olive oil over the top and sprinkle with the thyme, then the grated parmesan cheese. Cut the tomatoes in half and lay on the same tray cut side facing up. Drizzle the olive oil over the top. Season the tomatoes and mushrooms with salt and pepper and grill for 6–7 minutes or until the mushrooms have slightly collapsed and the parmesan is crisp and golden.

Meanwhile, in a medium frying pan, heat a drizzle of the olive oil over high heat, stab the clove of garlic with a fork and slide it, zigzagging over the pan, then set aside. This is a good way to get away with the essence of garlic for breakfast, without being too socially unacceptable! Toss the spinach leaves in the pan until they are just wilted, season with some salt and slide onto the tray with the tomato and mushrooms.

EGGS

Whisk the eggs, cream and salt and pepper to taste, together. Set aside.

Heat a medium non-stick frying pan over medium heat and melt the butter. Coat the entire pan and heat the butter until beginning to foam. Tip the egg mixture into the pan. It should immediately begin to cook. Using a spatula and starting on the edge closest to you, push the mixture, so the egg collects in folds on the opposite side. Now lift the pan off the heat and jiggle it around so the runny, uncooked mixture cascades to cover the entire pan again. As soon as the egg begins to cook again, repeat this pushing and jiggling technique. This will take literally seconds if you are doing it correctly. When you can feel the bottom of the mass of egg is just cooked and the top still quite runny, remove the pan from the heat, slide the eggs straight onto a plate and shave some parmesan over the top. Take it off any later and your eggs will be overcooked and you'll lose that silkiness you're after. It may take a few goes to get the timing right but even when these eggs are not perfect they are still pretty specky. Also, if you prefer, you may cook the eggs in 2 batches – 3 eggs to ¼ cup (60ml) of cream and use the same method as above.

Divide the grilled veggies between 2 plates and sprinkle some chopped parsley over the tomato, mushrooms and eggs. *Bon appétit!*

....

TIP: With the remaining sourdough loaf, you can slice the rest of the loaf thinly and freeze for your next sinful breakfast, or make thyme and parmesan croutons (see page 40).

....

While I was in Tasmania, I was lucky enough to visit wasabi grower, Matt Marston and his family. These beautiful chickens are part of his little slice of heaven.

eggs benedict

1½ tablespoons water

45ml white wine vinegar

3 egg yolks

200g unsalted butter, diced

pinch of white pepper

2 teaspoons lemon juice

¼ teaspoon salt, or to taste

700ml water

½ teaspoon salt

4 large free-range eggs, at room
temperature

2 English muffins, sliced in half,
toasted

butter, to spread

4 slices good quality ham

8 slices ripe tomato

This is one of my all time favourite breakfasts and I've recently discovered that it is also my dad's. Hollandaise, like all French white sauces, is the epitome of simplicity. Learning to make a good hollandaise was quite a culinary turning point for me in terms of understanding balance and flavour without a complex array of ingredients. It's also delicious and commonly served with blanched asparagus, white or green. If you're uncertain about how to time the poached eggs, sauce and toasted muffins so everything is warm, I suggest you make it a two-man job and engage a helper.

serves 2

To make the hollandaise, combine the water and vinegar in a small saucepan, and simmer until only half of the amount of liquid remains. Transfer the liquid to a stainless steel or glass mixing bowl and rest this over a saucepan half filled with hot water, so the bowl is not touching the water. Do not put the saucepan on the stove. Add the egg yolks and whisk madly, until the mixture is very light and fluffy. Add the cubes of butter, 1 or 2 at a time, continuing to whisk ferociously. You will notice the mixture getting beautifully thick and moussey after about 7 minutes. When you've emulsified all the butter into the mixture, add the pepper, lemon juice and salt. Taste a few times and adjust salt and the acid of the lemon juice accordingly. Cover and keep in a warm, not hot, spot on the stove.

In a medium frying pan or saucepan boil the water and salt, turn the heat off. Immediately crack 4 eggs, one at a time, into the boiled water. To make sure the eggs are fresh, with yolks intact, crack into a teacup before dropping each egg into the water. Poach for 4–5 minutes or until the whites are cooked and the yolks are still runny. Taking care not to break the yolks, remove the eggs with a slotted spoon or spatula and drain on a paper towel.

Just before you take your eggs out of the pan to drain, toast the muffins and butter them. Then pop a piece of ham and 2 slices of tomato on each half, add a poached egg on top and then the pièce de résistance – the hollandaise. Now close your eyes and savour every moment with your eggs benedict …

soft-boiled eggs with parmesan soldiers

1 loaf brioche

2 large free-range eggs, at room temperature

80g parmesan cheese, finely grated

1 teaspoon picked thyme leaves (optional)

1 tablespoon unsalted butter

drizzle of olive oil

2 large free-range eggs, whisked

I used to love soft-boiled eggs with soldiers as a kid. In Malaysia, we'd always have them only par boiled, with slightly runny whites, soy sauce, white pepper and heavily buttered white toast. It's a really lovely kiddy food memory I wanted to play on, so I thought why not parmesan soldiers. It's as naughty as eating fries for brekky. I promise there won't be a crumb in sight once breakfast is over.

serves 2

Slice the brioche into a few 2cm thick pieces. Trim crusts off and cut into exact 2 x 10cm batons. Cut 6 batons and set aside. Cut 2 squares 6 x 6cm from the remaining brioche slices and in the middle of each one, cut a round hole slightly larger than a 20 cent piece. The more precise the circle you cut, the better the result. This is going to be your edible eggcup.

Meanwhile, place the eggs in a small saucepan and fill with enough water to cover. Bring to the boil, boil for 3 minutes, drain and replace with cool water to prevent further cooking.

Mix the parmesan and thyme on a plate. Set aside. Melt the butter with a drizzle olive oil in a medium frying pan and heat over medium heat. Dip the batons and squares of brioche in the whisked eggs, then gently toss in the parmesan and thyme mixture to coat well. Cook on all sides, including the tips and edges, so each baton and square is perfectly golden brown and crispy. Arrange 3 batons and 1 square on each plate. Pop a drained egg in the hole of the square brioche, draw a smiley face on it and serve!

TIP: You may serve with clusters of oven roasted cherry tomatoes. Just bung them in the oven at 180°C for about 15 minutes with a drizzle of olive oil and a sprinkle of salt and pepper.

muffins

OK, if you've never baked in your life, this is definitely the place to start. It should be a no-brainer, and I hate to sound so ruthless but if you can't manage a muffin, I'm afraid your future as a baker is doomed! The process is as easy as it can get with baking – dump all the ingredients into a bowl and mix as little as you can get away with without leaving pockets of flour in the batter – you don't want to over work the gluten in the flour or you'll lose the lightness in your muffins. This is one of those recipes you can really have fun with as a beginner. Once you've successfully cooked this, go nuts experimenting with flavour combinations including savoury ones.

Basic muffin mix

2 cups (250g) plain flour, sifted

3 teaspoons baking powder, sifted

¾ cup (165g) brown sugar

½ teaspoon salt

85g unsalted butter, melted

1 large free-range egg, lightly whisked

½ cup (125ml) milk

⅓ cup (80ml) sour cream

1 teaspoon vanilla bean paste or natural vanilla extract

fruit or flavouring of your choice

basic muffin mix

makes 10-12

Heat the oven to 180°C (170°C fan forced). Line a 12-hole muffin pan with paper cases.

In a medium mixing bowl mix all the dry ingredients together. In a jug roughly mix the wet ingredients with the fruit or flavouring of your choice. Pour the wet ingredients over the dry ingredients and mix until just incorporated. Fill the paper cases almost to the top so the muffins generously bulge over the top when cooked. Bake on the middle shelf for 15–20 minutes, or until a skewer inserted in the centre of the muffin comes out clean.

BLUEBERRY MUFFINS

basic muffin mix

1½ cups fresh or frozen blueberries

blueberry muffins

makes 10-12

Using the basic muffin mix and method above, add the blueberries to the other wet ingredients.

TIP: Making your own self-raising flour is simple and I think far better in terms of consistency: add 1½ teaspoons of baking powder and a pinch of salt to 1 cup of plain flour.

LIME, ZUCCHINI AND DARK CHOCOLATE MUFFINS

basic muffin mix

1½ cups coarsely grated zucchini

zest of 2 limes or 1 orange

1 cup (150g) chopped good quality dark chocolate

lime, zucchini and dark chocolate muffins

makes 10–12

Heat the oven to 180°C (170°C fan forced). Line a 12-hole muffin pan with paper cases.

Follow the basic muffin mix recipe and mix all the dry ingredients together in a mixing bowl. In a jug roughly mix the wet ingredients with the zucchini, zest and chocolate. Pour the wet ingredients over the dry ingredients and mix until just incorporated. Fill the paper cases almost to the top so the muffins generously bulge over the top when cooked.

Bake on the middle shelf for 15–20 minutes, or until a skewer inserted in the centre of the muffin comes out clean.

BANANA AND DATE MUFFINS

Crumble

¼ cup (30g) plain flour

1 tablespoon brown sugar

½ teaspoon ground ginger

40g cold unsalted butter, cubed

½ cup (60g) pecans, chopped

Muffin

basic muffin mix

3 smallish or 2 large ripe bananas, diced into 1cm cubes

½ cup (80g) dried pitted dates, chopped

banana and date with pecan-ginger crumble muffins

makes 12

Heat the oven to 180°C (170°C fan forced). Line a 12-hole muffin pan with paper cases.

To make the crumble, blitz in a food processor the flour, sugar, ginger and butter to a crumble consistency. If the mixture seems too powdery, you need to pulse it further, so it is a little stickier. If doing by hand, rub the butter into the dry ingredients with your fingertips until there are no big chunks and it has a fine crumble consistency. Stir the nuts into the crumble. Set aside.

Follow the basic muffin mix recipe and mix all the dry ingredients together in a mixing bowl. In a jug roughly mix the wet ingredients with the bananas and dates. Pour the wet ingredients over the dry ingredients and mix until just incorporated. Don't completely fill the paper cases, fill to just 1cm below the top. Then scoop as much crumble as you can onto the top of the muffin mix so it is slightly domed but without making too much of a mess. Pat down gently.

Bake on the middle shelf for 15–20 minutes, or until a skewer inserted in the centre of the muffin comes out clean.

Crumble

¼ cup (30g) plain flour

1 tablespoon brown sugar

½ teaspoon cinnamon

40g cold unsalted butter, cubed

Muffin

basic muffin mix

1 cup green apple, peeled and diced into 1cm cubes

1 cup (125g) fresh or frozen raspberries

apple and raspberry with cinnamon crumble muffins

makes 12

Heat the oven to 180°C (170°C fan forced). Line a 12-hole muffin pan with paper cases.

To make the crumble, blitz in a food processor the flour, sugar, cinnamon and butter to a crumble consistency. If the mixture seems too powdery, you need to pulse it further, so it is a little stickier. If doing by hand, rub the butter into the dry ingredients with your fingertips until there are no big chunks and it has a fine crumble consistency. Set aside.

Follow the basic muffin mix recipe and mix all the dry ingredients together in a mixing bowl. In a jug roughly mix the wet ingredients with the apple and raspberries. Pour the wet ingredients over the dry ingredients and mix until just incorporated. Don't completely fill the paper cases, fill to just 1cm below the top. Then scoop as much crumble as you can onto the top of the muffin mix so it is slightly domed but without making too much of a mess. Pat down gently.

Bake on the middle shelf for 15–20 minutes, or until a skewer inserted in the centre of the muffin comes out clean.

2 cups (250g) plain flour, sifted

3 teaspoons baking powder, sifted

½ teaspoon salt

85g unsalted butter, melted

1 large free-range egg, lightly whisked

½ cup (125ml) milk

½ cup (125ml) sour cream

1½ cups coarsely grated zucchini

60g prosciutto, finely chopped

½ cup (50g) finely grated parmesan

½ cup (75g) grated mozzarella or tasty cheddar cheese

cheese and prosciutto muffins

makes 10–12

If you're not much of a sweet tooth, this one is for you.

Heat the oven to 180°C (170°C fan forced). Line a 12-hole muffin pan with paper cases.

In a medium mixing bowl mix all the dry ingredients together. In a jug roughly mix the wet ingredients with the zucchini, prosciutto and cheeses. Pour the wet ingredients over the dry ingredients and mix until just incorporated. Fill the paper cases almost to the top so the muffins generously bulge over the top when cooked.

Bake on the middle shelf for 15–20 minutes, or until a skewer inserted in the centre of the muffin comes out clean.

croissants

500g plain flour, sifted, plus extra
 for dusting

7g sachet or 1 teaspoon dry yeast

1 tablespoon lukewarm full cream
 milk

1¼–1⅓ cups (310–330ml) cold water

25g unsalted butter, melted

1½ teaspoons salt

¼ cup (55g) caster sugar

250g unsalted butter, softened

Egg wash

1 egg plus 1 egg yolk beaten with
 2½ tablespoons milk

This recipe is best made over two days to allow the dough to rest.

makes 12

Place the flour in a large bowl. Make a well in the centre and add the yeast and milk, stirring to dissolve. Wait a few minutes until the yeast mixture begins to bubble. Slowly add the water and melted butter and combine the ingredients gently with your fingertips. Add the salt and sugar and keep mixing with your fingers until the dough becomes very sticky. (You may need to add a little more water if the dough is not sticky enough.)

On a lightly floured surface, knead the dough with the palm of your hand, rolling it away from your body, for 8–10 minutes. Do not add any flour during the kneading. Place the dough in a bowl, cover the top with clingfilm and refrigerate overnight. It will double in size in the fridge.

Roll the dough into a rectangle about 5mm thick that is 3 times longer than it is wide. Spread half the softened butter over the centre third of the sheet. Fold the top third of the dough over the centre buttered section. Spread the remaining butter over the folded section, then fold the bottom third over the top.

Turn the dough 90 degrees so that the folded seams are at the sides. Roll the pastry again to form a large rectangular sheet and fold it in 3. Cover in clingfilm and refrigerate for 45 minutes.

Repeat the process of folding and refrigerating another 3 times – a total of 4 times.

Heat the oven to 220°C (220°C fan forced) and line a baking tray with baking paper.

Roll the dough into a large 5mm thick rectangle. (If you find the dough hard to manage, divide it into half.) Trim the edges, then cut into triangles 6–8cm wide x 12–15cm tall. Make a small triangular incision in the centre at the base of each triangle to allow the dough to stretch when being shaped. Starting from the widest end, roll the triangles up and shape into a crescent.

Space the croissants out on the baking tray and leave them to rise by about one-third in a draft-free, warm room (21°C is ideal) for about an hour.

When the croissant have risen, brush them with the egg wash and bake for 10 minutes, or until golden. Do not open the oven door during cooking time. Transfer to a wire rack to cool.

12 x 1 day-old croissants
(see previous pages)

Crème patissiere

(Makes about 1 cup/250ml)

200ml full cream milk

½ vanilla bean, split lengthways and seeds scraped

3 egg yolks

¼ cup (50g) caster sugar

2 tablespoons plain flour, sifted

20g unsalted butter, diced

Crème d'amande

(Makes about 3 cups)

150g unsalted butter, softened and diced

1¼ cups (155g) icing sugar, sifted

1½ cups (155g) almond meal

2 tablespoons cornflour, sifted

3 egg yolks

2 drops amaretto liqueur

1 cup (250g) crème patissiere

Syrup

1 cup (250ml) water

½ cup (110g) sugar

kirsch (optional)

flaked almonds, to decorate

icing sugar, to dust

almond croissants

Almond croissants, my way. This is a perfect way to use day-old croissants, the ones you didn't manage to eat on the first day.

makes 12

First make the crème patissiere. Combine the milk and vanilla bean and seeds in a saucepan and bring to the boil. Meanwhile, in a mixing bowl (or electric mixer), whisk the egg yolks and sugar until the mixture is fluffy and pale, forming thick ribbons when drizzled from the whisk. Add the flour and mix well. Stir the hot milk into the egg mixture and mix well again. Using a fine sieve, strain the cream mixture back into the saucepan, discarding the vanilla bean and any lumps. Cook on low heat for 3–5 minutes until the mixture thickens, whisking continuously to prevent the mixture sticking to the pan. Transfer the mixture to a mixing bowl, add the butter, combine well, set aside to cool. Cover the surface of the cream with a layer of clingfilm to avoid a skin forming.

To make the crème d'amande, beat the butter, icing sugar, almond meal and cornflour in an electric mixer on medium speed until pale and creamy. Add the egg yolks one by one, mixing well each time.

Add the liqueur and the crème patissiere, mix well with a wooden spoon to combine. Set aside until required.

Preheat the oven to 180°C (170°C fan forced). Grease 2 large baking trays and line with baking paper.

To make the syrup, place the water and sugar in a small saucepan over medium heat, stirring until the sugar dissolves. Bring to the boil and add a splash of kirsch, if you want.

Cut the croissants with a serrated knife and brush generously with the syrup.

Spread some crème d'amande on one half of each of the croissants, put the other half on top and spread on more crème d'amande. Sprinkle the flaked almonds on top.

Place the croissants on the prepared trays. Lay a sheet of baking paper on top of the croissants, then place an extra tray on top to flatten (almond croissants always cook between 2 trays). Bake for 15–20 minutes, or until crisp and golden.

Remove the trays, let the croissants cool down completely, then dust with the icing sugar and voila ...

— Emmanuel Mollois

Emmanuel on his bike outside his cafe in Perth, Western Australia.

Emmanuel Mollois

Emmanuel Mollois is a delight to work with. He's very earnest, very enthusiastic and a Frenchman who's very proud to be Australian. To illustrate his good humour, he tells me with hands over his face and a big smile that his children eat croissants with vegemite. Our relationship is always peppered with loads of laughter and mischief.

Culturally we couldn't be further from one another. I'm always frustrating him with my unorthodox ways. And while he perpetually wows me with his gorgeous, traditional pastries, I'm always trying to shock his French palate with my brand of Asian … perhaps the durian dumplings were a step too far. With his discipline and my lack of it (but I'd like to think of it as being an abundance of creativity), we're constantly cross-pollinating with methods we learn from one another. This has made for a great friendship in the kitchen.

FUN FACTS:

• The slightest bit of chilli will blow Emmanuel's head off.

• He loves his family but also music, drumming, cycling, war artefacts and sugar — there's a reason why he's a pastry chef!

• He always refers to whatever he's doing as 'him'. For instance, 'Whisk eem until ee is very thick'.

That day I had just done my deep-fried meringue with pandan crème patissiere and Emmanuel had made chocolate eclairs. If I never make it to Paris, at least I've tasted one of Emmanuel's chocolate eclairs!

crepes

Crepe batter (makes 8-9 crepes)

⅓ cup (40g) plain flour

2 large free-range eggs

¾ cup (190ml) whole milk

pinch salt

1 tablespoon vegetable oil or melted butter

1 teaspoon natural vanilla extract (omit for savoury crepes)

butter, softened to grease pan

My absolute favourite way to eat these is with good Canadian maple syrup and a dollop of cream (see page 175).

serves 4

Pop a non-stick frying pan on a low heat to begin warming.

In a medium mixing bowl, combine the flour, eggs, ¼ cup of milk, salt, oil or melted butter and whisk until silky smooth. Add a little more milk and whisk until nicely incorporated. Mix the remaining milk in with a ladle to avoid incorporating too much air into the batter. The mixture should be quite watery. If the consistency is right, the batter will split into droplets when poured from the ladle in a slow stream, but if it forms a smooth band of liquid, your crepes will end up too thick.

Heat a 20–23cm non-stick frying pan over medium heat. To test, ladle a droplet of batter into the pan, if it sizzles and instantly bubbles, it's probably a bit too hot. Just grab the pan and making sure no one is around you, madly wave it around to cool it down a tad. Return to the stove, and with some paper towels, smear butter over the entire surface of the pan. Ladle a ¼ cup of the batter into the pan, roll it around to cover the surface. You have to work quickly, as it will begin to cook instantly. When the crepe is perfect, the edge will crisp up and become golden. At this point lift up an edge with a butter knife, then with both hands, carefully pick it up and swiftly flip it over. Cook it for literally a second on the other side, then flip it onto a plate. Repeat until all the mixture is used. You should end up with crepes that are about 1mm thick and transluscent. If they are too thick, it means you are either pouring too much mixture into the pan and letting the excess settle instead of pouring it out, or your batter needs thinning with more milk.

lemon and sugar – an old faithful

LEMON AND SUGAR

1 crepe

4 lemon wedges

8 teaspoons caster sugar

A good squeeze of lemon, sprinkle of sugar, roll the crepe up and wolf it down. A light drizzle of cream just before rolling it up is also delish!

chocolate hazelnut spread – Parisian favourite

CHOCOLATE HAZELNUT SPREAD

4 tablespoons chocolate hazelnut spread

A good slather of chocolate hazelnut spread from a spatula is how Parisians usually eat their crepes from street vendors.

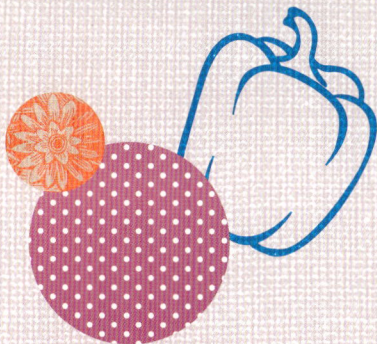

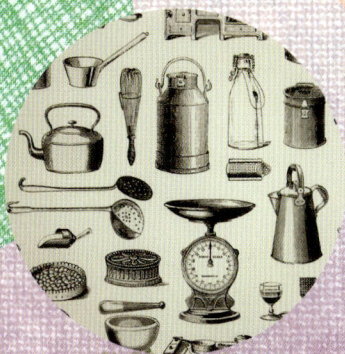

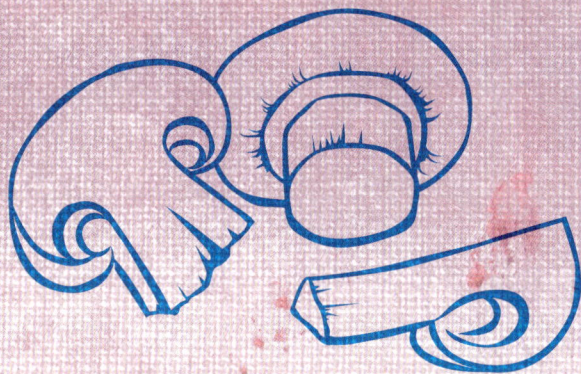

soups

pumpkin and roasted red capsicum

1½ tablespoons olive oil

25g butter

2 medium brown onions, finely
chopped

650g pumpkin, diced into 1cm cubes
(see tip below)

1 large red capsicum, char-grilled,
peeled and roughly chopped
(see note below)

2 cups (500ml) chicken stock
(see page 49)

1 teaspoon salt or to taste

¼ teaspoon freshly cracked black
pepper

2 teaspoons fresh lemon juice

sour cream or crème fraîche lightly
whisked to loosen

Soups must be one of the easiest dishes to serve in winter. Quick, good for freezing, and fantastic for using up surplus vegetables that are in season. The thing I love most is that if you make them nice and hearty, they are substantial enough for a meal. On your way home from work, just remember to grab some gorgeous loaves of artisan-style bread (there's nothing as delectable as a complete surrender to carbs on a winter night), and then splurge on some high quality French butter to go with it. This particular recipe I came up with for dinner after rummaging around in my vegetable crisper. You can use it as a mother recipe. This means if you omit the pumpkin, red capsicum and lemon juice, you can use the rest to make any soup by substituting different vegetables (like the celery over the page) and adding some cream at the end if you wish. Go nuts!

serves 4

In a non-stick pot, melt the butter with the olive oil. Add the onions and cook on a medium heat until tender but uncoloured. Add the pumpkin and capsicum and sauté for a minute or two before adding the stock. Bring to the boil and then simmer until the pumpkin is tender. Blitz the mixture in an electric blender or with a stick blender until smooth. Stir in salt, pepper and lemon juice. Serve with a dollop of sour cream or crème fraîche.

NOTE: To char-grill and remove the skin from a capsicum, first remove the stem and seeds, then slice down one side of the capsicum, grab either side of the cut and open up the capsicum. Lie the capsicum down with skin facing up on a baking tray lined with foil. Squash down (you can be quite rough) the capsicum as flat as it will go. Grill on high heat, as close to the grill as you can get, until the skin is blistered black all over. Remove the tray from the grill, gather up the foil and wrap up the capsicum so you have a sealed parcel. Allow it to sit for 5–10 minutes. You'll find the sweating will make the charred skin very easy to peel off.

TIP: Dicing veggies into small cubes means they will cook very quickly and therefore save time and maintain their vitality.

cream of celery

60g butter

1 tablespoon olive oil

2 medium brown onions, finely chopped

1 bunch celery including leaves, chopped very finely

4 cups (1 litre) chicken stock (see page 49)

¾ cup (190ml) milk

¾ cup (190ml) pouring cream

1 teaspoon salt or to taste

¼ teaspoon freshly cracked white or black pepper

2 tablespoon chopped chives

I feel cream of everything else gets more attention than this blast from the past which I just love. Apart from being one of the usual suspects in a selection of crudités, I feel celery is a horribly neglected vegetable, but here it is given a rare opportunity to shine!

serves 6

In a non-stick pot, melt the butter with the olive oil. Add the onions and cook on a medium heat for 2 minutes or until tender and slightly golden. Add the celery and sauté for a minute or two before adding in the stock and milk. Bring to the boil and then simmer for 15 minutes or until the celery is very tender. Blitz in an electric blender or with a stick blender until smooth. If you find the mixture a little fibrous, pass through a sieve.

Return to the pot, add cream, salt and pepper. Reheat and serve with a sprinkle of chopped chives.

cream of cauliflower

25g butter

1½ tablespoons olive oil

2 medium brown onions, chopped

½ head of cauliflower, with stalk, finely chopped

1½ cups (375ml) chicken stock (see page 49)

1 cup (250ml) full cream milk

¼ cup (60ml) pouring cream

1 teaspoon salt or to taste

¼ teaspoon freshly cracked white pepper

freshly grated nutmeg (optional)

An oldie but a goodie.

serves 6

In a non-stick pot, melt the butter with the olive oil. Add the onions and cook on a medium heat for 2 minutes or until tender but uncoloured. Add the cauliflower and sauté for a minute or two before adding in the stock and milk. Bring to the boil and then simmer for 15 minutes or until the cauliflower is very tender. Blitz in an electric blender or with a stick blender until smooth. If you find the mixture a little fibrous, pass through a sieve.

Return to the pot, add cream, salt and pepper. Reheat and serve with a grating of nutmeg over each bowl.

chunky cream of mushroom

The 'chunk' is what makes this a little different to your usual cream of mushroom but if you insist, just blitz away at the end of the recipe for a more velvety finish.

serves 6

60g butter

1 tablespoon olive oil

3 cloves garlic, finely chopped

4 spring onions, chopped

1 teaspoon thyme, picked

800g mixed large swiss browns and button mushrooms

4 cups (1 litre) chicken stock (see page 49)

¾ cup (190ml) cream

1 teaspoon table salt OR to taste (double if using sea salt flakes)

¼ teaspoon freshly cracked white or black pepper

3 teaspoons chopped parsley

thyme and parmesan croutons (optional)

In a non-stick saucepan, melt the butter with the olive oil. Add the garlic and the spring onions and cook over a medium heat for 1–2 minutes, or until the garlic is fragrant but still uncoloured, and the spring onions wilted. Add thyme, sauté for 1 minute, then add the mushrooms. Sauté for about 5 minutes or until some of the mushrooms are golden and the rest wilted, before adding in the stock. Bring to the boil and then add cream. Remove half the soup and blend in an electric blender or with a stick blender. Return to the rest of the soup and stir through. If you prefer a regular cream of mushroom, blend all the soup for a velvety finish. Reheat and add salt and pepper. Sprinkle with chopped parsley and serve, with thyme and parmesan croutons.

THYME AND PARMESAN CROUTONS

(see note below)

1 baguette (French stick) or any robust artisan-style loaf like a sourdough or Turkish pide

olive oil

1 bunch thyme

¾–1 cup grated parmesan cheese

thyme and parmesan croutons

Set oven to 180°C (170°C fan forced).

If you're using a baguette, with a very sharp chef's knife, slice very thinly 2–3mm thick, on the diagonal. This can be very time consuming and you do need knife skills. Lay each piece on a baking tray lined with baking paper and brush each piece with olive oil. Sprinkle plucked thyme leaves and a little shaved parmesan over each piece. Bake for about 10 minutes or until the parmesan cheese is golden and the bread is beautifully crisp.

If you want to do it the quick way, just break your artisan loaf into uniform 3cm chunks (if they are not the same size, some will remain soft while others will bake to a cinder) and place on a baking tray lined with baking paper. Drizzle a decent amount of olive oil over the top and lightly toss with your hands to evenly distribute the oil. Pluck a few sprigs of thyme, grab a handful of the parmesan and sprinkle generously over the pieces of bread. Bake on the middle rack for about 20–30 minutes, but do keep an eye on them to make sure they don't burn. They should be beautifully golden and super crispy. Sprinkle over the soup of your choice.

NOTE: These quantities will make you quite a lot, but you can cool, then freeze them, and reheat in the oven when needed.

red lentil and tomato soup

2 tablespoons olive oil

2 cloves garlic, finely chopped

1 large brown onion, chopped

2 medium slices prosciutto, chopped
    into 1cm squares (optional)

½–1 teaspoon dried chilli flakes

1 teaspoon mustard powder

2 carrots, diced 2cm cubes

3 medium tomatoes skinned (see
    note below) and roughly chopped
    (if desperate, use canned but
    fresh is far superior)

4 cups (1 litre) chicken stock
    (see page 49)

100g red lentils, rinsed

juice of ½ lemon

½ teaspoon salt or to taste

¼ teaspoon freshly cracked white
    or black pepper

This is one of my faithfully quick dinner recipes which can be bulked up further with some shredded chicken for the carnivores.

serves 4

In a non-stick medium saucepan heat the olive oil on medium and sweat the garlic and onion until they are tender but uncoloured. Add the prosciutto and chilli, mustard powder and sauté to render some fat off the prosciutto and until the flesh is a little crispy. Add the carrots and sauté for 3 minutes or until they are softened. Add the tomatoes, stock and lentils and simmer for 15–20 minutes or until the lentils are tender.

Turn off the heat and add the lemon juice. Season with salt and pepper.

Serve with a nice crusty loaf.

NOTE: To skin tomatoes, first remove the stems and tops. With a small paring knife, score the skin of each tomato all the way around. Place the tomatoes in a bowl and cover with boiling water. Weigh the tomatoes down with a small saucer and wait for 5–10 minute. Drain and the skins should almost fall off or at least be peeled very easily. Chop roughly and set aside.

watermelon rind with glass vermicelli

2 tablespoons vegetable oil

400g green medium prawns, peeled and deveined, shells and heads reserved

8 cups (2 litres) water

3 red eschalots roughly chopped

10g belachan (see note below)

rind from ¼ watermelon, green skin cut off and cut into 3cm squares

4 bird's-eye chillies, cut in half lengthways and deseeded

5 white peppercorns, crushed

½ teaspoon sugar

1–1½ tablespoons fish sauce, or to taste

200g dry glass vermicelli

coriander sprigs, to garnish

....

NOTE: Squash the belachan on a double layer of foil. Wrap to seal and roast in the oven for 10 minutes at 180°C, or until the belachan is dry, crumbly and pungent.

....

I came across this recipe about a year ago in an old Nonya cookbook and instantly fell in love with it as it speaks so highly of the resourcefulness of Nonya women, by turning something that would usually go in the bin into this very clever dish. The watermelon rind pieces, as novel as they seem, are not just scraps floating superfluously in the soup. In fact, they have the beautiful subtle flavour of a lot of gourds the Chinese like to use in their soups and the little flashes of red flesh that remain on the rind are visually very charming. I will however, warn you that this soup is very prawny in the way that Southeast Asian dishes that contain belachan can be.

serves 4–6

To make the stock, heat the oil in a large saucepan over medium-high heat. Stir-fry the prawn shells and heads for 7 minutes, or until fragrant and golden. Add the water and bring to the boil. Cover and boil for 5 minutes, reduce the heat to low, and simmer for 20 minutes. Strain the stock and discard the shells.

To make the prawn mixture, pound the eschalots, prawns and belachan in a mortar and pestle until a coarse paste or if you're lazy, pulse in a food processor. Add the prawn mixture to the stock, cover and bring back to boil for another 10 minutes.

Add the watermelon rind, chillies, peppercorns, sugar and fish sauce. Cook for another 10 minutes, or until the rind is tender. Turn the heat off and cover.

Meanwhile, place the vermicelli in a large bowl. Pour in enough boiling water to cover the noodles. Cover and leave for 5 minutes, or until tender. Drain. Divide the noodles between serving bowls and ladle the hot soup over the top. Garnish with coriander and serve immediately.

beetroot borscht with pirozhki

50g butter

1 large brown onion, chopped

4 cloves garlic, chopped

500g beetroot, peeled and diced into 1cm cubes

2 medium carrots, peeled and thinly diced

6 cups (1.5 litres) beef stock (see page 49)

1½ tablespoons plain flour

¾ cup (180ml) tomato puree, bottled passata or tinned crushed tomatoes

300g desiree potatoes peeled and diced into 1cm cubes

2½ tablespoons balsamic vinegar

1 teaspoon sugar

1 teaspoon salt or to taste

¼ teaspoon freshly cracked white or black pepper

sour cream or crème fraîche, lightly whisked to loosen

4 tablespoons chopped flat-leaf parsley

I've always been fascinated with Eastern European food but borscht and any dumplings from that part of the world, I'm a complete sucker for. I'm not sure whether it's the colour or the fact that I never ate beetroot growing up or that there are so many versions of borscht across Eastern Europe. This recipe paired with the pirozhki is positively heavenly. I have to admit that with the beef stock it's a fair amount of work but I promise it's worth the trouble. It's one of these dishes that makes you swell with pride when you've taken the trouble. I promise, it's worth it.

serves 6

Heat the butter in a large non-stick saucepan on medium heat. Sweat the onion and garlic for 2 minutes or until soft but not coloured. Add the beetroot and carrot and sauté until tender, then pour in the beef stock. While this is heating up on the stove, whisk the plain flour into 3 tablespoons of the passata, when combined, whisk in the rest of the passata. Add the passata mixture to the soup mixture. Cover and bring to the boil. Add the potatoes, balsamic vinegar and sugar. Simmer for 15-20 minutes or until the potatoes and beetroot are tender and then add the salt and pepper. Blend in an electric blender or with a stick blender until silky smooth.

Serve with a generous dollop of sour cream or crème fraîche swirled through the borscht, a sprinkle of parsley and the pirozhki.

Filling

40g butter

1 tablespoon olive oil

7 red eschalots (70g) or 1 large
onion, chopped

2 cloves garlic, finely chopped

160g of a combination of cabbage,
mushrooms and carrot, finely
chopped

300g chicken, beef or pork mince

½ teaspoon caraway seeds

1 teaspoon paprika

2 hard boiled eggs, chopped

3 tablespoons chopped flat-leaf
parsley

1 teaspoon salt or to taste

¼ teaspoon freshly cracked white
or black pepper

Sour cream shortcrust pastry

2⅔ cups (335g) plain flour

1 teaspoon baking powder

1 teaspoon salt or to taste

180g cold unsalted butter, diced

2 egg yolks

½ cup (125ml) sour cream

1–2 tablespoons cold water if
neccessary

1 large free-range egg beaten
(for egg wash)

pirozhki

makes approximately 18

FILLING

To make the filling, melt the butter with the olive oil in a frying pan on medium heat and sweat the eschalots and garlic so they are fragrant but uncoloured. Add the chopped vegetables and sauté for 2–3 minutes or until they are tender. Add the meat, caraway seeds and paprika and sauté until the meat is cooked.

To complete, add the egg, parsley, salt and pepper. Stir until combined, then spread out on a dinner plate to cool completely before using.

SOUR CREAM SHORTCRUST PASTRY

Set the oven to 200°C (190°C fan-forced).

Combine the flour, baking powder, salt, butter, yolks and sour cream in a large food processor and pulse until the mixture starts to form a ball. If it seems excessively crumbly and isn't coming together, add a tablespoon of cold water. Tip the contents onto the bench and knead briefly to collect any stray crumbs. Divide the dough in half, roll each half into a ball, and press down to form a thick disc. Cover both discs with clingfilm and refrigerate for 30 minutes.

To assemble the pirozhki, take one of the discs out of the fridge, unwrap and place on a lightly floured bench top. Bash a few times with the rolling pin in different spots to loosen the dough a little before rolling out to 3mm thick. Dust a 10cm pastry cutter with flour and cut as many circles as you can out of the pastry. Continue to roll and cut until all the dough is used. Place on each circle of pastry a tablespoon of cooled filling, fold in half, brush the edge with a little egg wash and press all around with the tip of a fork to seal the crescent shaped parcel. Place on a baking tray lined with baking paper, leave a 2cm space between each pirozhki. Place the tray of pirozhkis in the freezer for 10 minutes. Repeat with the other discs of dough.

With a pastry brush, coat all the pirozhkis liberally with the egg wash. This will ensure a beautiful golden finish.

Turn oven down to 180°C (170°C fan forced) and bake for 15–20 minutes or until the pastry is deep golden. Serve immediately with a bowl of borscht.

soup stock

CHICKEN STOCK

2kg organic chicken carcass bones

3.5 litres water.

easy-peasy chicken stock

makes 1.5 litres

I always make a neutral chicken stock which has no herbs in it as I prefer the versatility of being able to use it for both Asian and European dishes. This being the case, it's a very casual affair of cramming as many raw chicken carcasses (easily available from the local chicken shop or butcher) into a stock pot, as you can. I usually fit about 6 in mine. Cover with the water and simply bring to the boil uncovered and then lower the heat to a gentle simmer. After 30 minutes grab a ladle or tongs to collapse the carcasses, pushing them down so they are well submerged. Continue cooking 2–2$1/2$ hours, skimming the frothy impurities off the top as you go. Remove the bones, strain through a sieve, cool and refrigerate so all the fat solidifies and is easy to remove. Freeze surplus stock.

BEEF STOCK

2kg beef bones

2 carrots, roughly chopped

2 medium brown onions with skins, roughly chopped

3 litres water

2 sticks celery with tops, roughly chopped

1 bouquet garni (2 sprigs parsley, 2 sprigs thyme and 1 bay leaf)

10–12 black peppercorns

....

TIP: Freeze your stock in batches already measured out for later convenience

....

beef stock

makes approximately 1.5 litres

Bear with me on this one. Beef stock is time consuming but I'm afraid there's no short cut to a good beef stock. The only consolation is that I recommend you make double the amount to make it worth your while. And like so many of the lessons with cooking, once you've done it a few times, you won't bat an eyelid at the 5 hour cooking time … was that convincing enough?

Set the oven to 210°C (200°C fan forced) and bake the bones in a roasting dish for 30 minutes. Add the carrots and onions and bake for another 20 minutes. Transfer the contents of the roasting dish to a large stock pot and pile in the remaining ingredients. Bring to the boil, then lower the heat and simmer uncovered for 4 hours, skimming the frothy impurities off the top as you go. Strain the stock through a fine sieve to remove any solids, then discard all the solids.

Cool and refrigerate so all the fat solidifies on the top, which makes it easy to remove. Freeze any surplus stock for later.

fish

salmon with almond sauce, buckwheat tuile and herb salad

4 x 180g salmon fillets, skin on

olive oil, for cooking

Buckwheat tuiles

½ cup (65g) buckwheat flour, sifted

1½ tablespoons sugar

1 teaspoons salt

100g egg white (approximately
    3 egg whites)

50ml pouring cream

100g clarified butter

Almond sauce
    (makes approximately
    1 cup/250ml)

2 teaspoons olive oil

1 small brown onion, finely chopped

1 cup (100g) almond meal

100ml dry white wine

100ml full cream milk

200ml pouring cream

Herb salad

1 cup flat leaf parsley leaves

½ cup dill

¾ cup fresh tarragon

120g mixed lettuce leaves

juice of 1 lemon

100ml of extra virgin olive oil

This recipe is very easy and looks amazing with lots of colours. It is best to make the tuile mix the day before.

serves 4

To make the buckwheat tuiles, heat the oven to 170°C (160°C fan forced). Grease 2 large baking trays and line with baking paper.

In a medium-sized bowl, combine buckwheat flour, sugar and salt, then add the egg whites, cream and clarified butter and mix until well combined.

Drop level tablespoons of the mixture onto the prepared trays, allowing 4 per tray. Spread the mixture out thinly to make a 10cm circle. Bake for 8–10 minutes, or until golden. Repeat to make at least 12 tuiles.

To make the almond milk, heat a small saucepan over medium heat, add the oil and cook the onion for 1–2 minutes until soft but not coloured. Add the almond meal. Pour in the wine to deglaze, and allow to reduce by half, then pour in the milk and cream. Cook for 2–3 minutes, or until the almond meal is soft.

Let the sauce cool a little and then blend until smooth. Season with salt and pepper to taste, then strain through a fine sieve. It is fine if the sauce is still a bit frothy. Set aside until ready to serve.

To make the herb salad, toss the herbs and lettuce leaves in a large bowl. Whisk together the lemon juice and olive oil, dress and season the salad just before serving.

To cook the salmon, heat a frying pan over high heat until the pan is very hot. Add the olive oil, and cook skin side down for 2–3 minutes. Reduce the heat to low, and continue cooking the fish for a further 2 minutes, or until medium rare. Do not turn the fish.

To serve, place the salmon on serving plates. Beside the salmon alternate the tuiles with the herb salad, allowing 3 tuiles per serve. Put the almond sauce in a small pot alongside the fish.

— *Emmanuel Mollois*

poached whiting with beurre blanc

4 whiting fillets, 8 if small, bones removed with tweezers

Beurre blanc

½ cup (125ml) white wine

¼ cup (60ml) white wine vinegar

1 red eschalot, very finely chopped

100g unsalted butter, chopped into small cubes and softened

2 teaspoons lemon juice

½ teaspoon salt, or to taste

pinch of white pepper

Court bouillon

1 cup (250ml) water

¾ cup (185ml) dry white wine

1 small onion, sliced

1 bay leaf

1 fennel frond

5 black peppercorns

1 parsley of sprig

¼ teaspoon salt

1 piece lemon peel

Many years ago I was not at all acquainted with the French obsession with cooking fish perfectly. The first time I tasted this recipe was definitely one of those culinary light bulb moments that seemed to make my mind go soft with pleasure. It's the most ingenious, seamless transition from delicate flesh to buttery sauce, and is a great example of balance at the quiet end of the spectrum, which the French are brilliant at.

serves 4

To make the beurre blanc, place the white wine, vinegar and eschalot in a small saucepan and simmer until the liquid is reduced to just over 1 tablespoon and the eschalot is tender. Remove from the heat and allow to cool for about 5 minutes.

Adding only a few cubes at a time, whisk the butter into the reduction until emulsified. If the butter is melting very quickly, whisk madly and allow the mixture to cool for another minute. Keep doing this until all the butter has been incorporated and you have a thick, smooth, yellow sauce. For a more refined sauce, press the contents through a sieve. Add the lemon juice and season with salt and white pepper, and set aside in a warm place.

If you wish, you can vary this by adding a couple of tablespoons of capsicum puree (see over page), or a few drops of Tabasco sauce for a subtle kick of heat.

To poach the fish, place all the ingredients for the court bouillon in a frying pan with a lid and bring to the boil. Turn the heat off, but keep on the stove and allow bouillon to cool for 10 seconds. Place the fish in the bouillon (the fish should be entirely covered or only fall short by a couple of millimetres) and cover with a lid. Leave for 5-6 minutes, or until the fish is just cooked. If your fillets are large, cook 2 fillets at a time but you will have to reheat the bouillon for each batch.

Plate immediately, spooning 1-2 tablespoons of beurre blanc over each fillet.

Serve with stringless green beans with slivered almonds.

**GREEN BEANS WITH
SLIVERED ALMONDS**

2–3 tablespoons slivered almonds

300g stringless green beans, topped but not tailed – the tails are harmless and cute

25g unsalted butter

1 teaspoon lemon juice

sea salt and freshly cracked black pepper

green beans with slivered almonds

Toast the slivered almonds in a frying pan over medium heat until lightly golden.

In a saucepan, boil the beans in salted water for 1–2 minutes, so they still have some crunch. If in doubt, taste to check the texture. Drain and transfer to a serving dish. Toss in the butter until the beans are coated. Squeeze a wedge of lemon over the top, season with the salt and pepper, and sprinkle the slivered almonds over the top.

capsicum puree

Take one capsicum and remove the stem. Slice down one side of the capsicum, grab either side of the cut and splay the capsicum open. Lie skin facing up on a baking tray lined with foil and further squash down (you may be quite rough) the capsicum so it is as flat as it will go. Grill on high heat and as close to the grill as you can get, until the skin is blistered black all over. Remove from the grill, gather the sides of the foil together and scrunch up so you have a sealed parcel. Allow it to sit for 5–10 minutes. You'll find the sweating will make the charred skin very easy to peel off. Chop into small pieces and puree with a stick blender. Run the puree through a sieve. At the very end of the process of making the beurre blanc, whisk the puree through.

A Chinese fishing village on the island of Penang. The villagers actually live in clans in houses built on piers.

Szechuan-style whole snapper with woodear fungus

1 x 1kg whole red snapper or any white fleshed fish, cleaned

4 cups (1 litre) peanut or vegetable oil

2 spring onions, finely sliced

coriander sprigs, to garnish

steamed jasmine rice, to serve

Marinade

1 tablespoon shaoxing rice wine

1 tablespoon finely chopped ginger

½ teaspoon salt

Sauce

2-3 tablespoons peanut or vegetable oil

4 cloves garlic, finely chopped

2 tablespoons finely chopped ginger

3 spring onions, finely sliced on the diagonal

2 tablespoons toban jiang (chilli bean paste)

15g woodear fungus, soaked in cool water for 15 minutes, woody parts discarded, finely shredded

1 tablespoon shaoxing rice wine

1 tablespoon light soy sauce

2 teaspoons sugar

1 tablespoon Chinese black vinegar

1½ cups (375ml) water

1 tablespoon cornflour

Toban jiang or chilli bean paste is one of those ingredients that magically transforms a dish. It injects a certain depth of flavour into a dish with very little effort. The combination of the salty, spicy chilli bean paste, the acidity of the black vinegar, the crunch of the woodear fungus with that classic Chinese trinity of garlic, ginger and spring onions makes for an intriguingly delicious sauce to go with fish. If you're still a little afraid of deep frying a whole fish, you can use fillets, using the same method.

serves 2 or 4-6 as a shared meal

At 2cm intervals, score the fish with a knife diagonally right through to the bone.

To make the marinade, mix the shaoxing, ginger and the salt. Place the fish in a dish and massage thoroughly with the marinade. Cover with clingfilm and set aside in a cool place for 30 minutes.

To make the sauce, heat the oil in a frying pan to medium-high. Add the garlic, ginger, spring onions and sauté for a few seconds until fragrant, before adding the toban jiang. Stir-fry for a few seconds, then add the woodear fungus, shaoxing, soy sauce, sugar and black vinegar. Cook for another few seconds, then add the water. Scoop out a couple of tablespoons of the sauce and mix with the cornflour until there are no lumps. Add the cornflour mixture to the wok and stir while bringing to the boil. Turn the heat down and season further with salt if required. Transfer the sauce to a small saucepan, cover and set aside.

To cook the fish, fill the wok with the oil and heat to medium-high. To test if the oil is ready, insert a wooden spoon or chopstick into the oil. If the oil bubbles up from the wood, it is ready. Pat the fish thoroughly dry with some paper towels, as any moisture will cause severe spitting. Hold the fish by its tail and slide in gently. If the fish isn't completely immersed, use a Chinese cooking ladle to gently baste the fish with oil until it is cooked. It should take 8-10 minutes, but if in doubt, remove the fish from the oil, make a small incision at the thickest part of the fish and check whether the flesh resting on the bone is cooked. Drain the fish on a paper towel. Transfer the fish to a plate and sprinkle on the spring onions.

Meanwhile, reheat the sauce and immediately pour over fish. Garnish with the sprigs of coriander and serve with steamed jasmine rice.

classic Chinese steamed fish – Cantonese style

1 x 1kg whole white fish (barramundi, baby red snapper, coral trout), cleaned

2 tablespoons peanut or vegetable oil

freshly ground white pepper

2 tablespoons finely shredded ginger

a dozen coriander sprigs

2–3 spring onions, shredded diagonally (soak in ice water if you want beautiful curly tendrils but not necessary)

steamed jasmine rice, to serve

Marinade

1½ tablespoons shaoxing rice wine

2 tablespoons light soy sauce

1 tablespoon finely chopped ginger

1 teaspoon sesame oil

This is truly an unbeatable way to eat fish and this recipe will give you that classic steamed fish you find eating out but can never seem to replicate at home. It's ridiculously simple and the trick is all in the final flourish when you pour that scalding peanut oil over the fish, blistering the skin and scalding the aromas – the fragrance released is unforgettable.

serves 2 or 4–6 as a shared meal

Place the fish on a large plate and make three slits to the bone 3cm apart on both sides of the fish. Spoon over the marinade of shaoxing, soy, ginger and sesame oil, massage gently over the entire fish. Clingfilm and marinate in the fridge for 10 minutes.

Balance the plate of fish on a metal trivet in a wok and steam, covered with a domed lid, for 5–8 minutes, or until the fish is cooked. To test if the fish is cooked, insert a small sharp knife into the thickest part of the flesh and part gently. If the flesh is translucent, it is cooked. Remove the plate from the wok and set aside.

Heat the peanut or vegetable oil in a hot wok until it smokes. Sprinkle the fish with pepper, shredded ginger, coriander and spring onions, then slowly pour the hot oil over the fish to crisp the skin and scald the aromatics. Serve with steamed jasmine rice.

NOTE: Before I overcame my fear of steaming and dealing with whole fish, I used to do this dish in the oven set at 150°C (140°C fan forced) by wrapping the fish fillets and the juice from the marinade in foil and placing it on a baking tray. Then I would bake it for 8–10 minutes and follow-up with the same finishing as described above.

steamed Moroccan snapper

4 x 200g snapper steaks

½ cup (125ml) chermoula

juice of 1 lemon

2 tablespoons honey

sea salt

½ cup (125ml) water

1 preserved lemon (see next page), quartered, pith removed and rind finely sliced

2 tablespoons chopped coriander leaves

Chermoula
(makes approximately 2 cups/500ml)

1 red onion, roughly chopped

4 cloves garlic, roughly chopped

1 bunch coriander, with stalks, washed and roughly chopped

1 bunch flat-leaf parsley, with stalks, washed and roughly chopped

1 heaped teaspoon sea salt

1 tablespoon ground cumin

1 tablespoon ground coriander

1½ tablespoons chilli powder

1 tablespoon ground turmeric

½ tablespoon sweet paprika

1½ tablespoons ras el hanouts (optional)

¾ cup (185ml) extra virgin olive oil

juice of 1 lemon

serves 4

First, make the chermoula.

Put all the ingredients in a food processor, except the olive oil and lemon juice. Process for 1 minute, then slowly pour in the olive oil until a thick paste forms. Stir through the lemon juice. If making ahead, refrigerate until ready to use.

In a stainless steel bowl, mix the fish with the chermoula and leave to marinate for 1 hour.

Transfer the fish to a shallow ceramic bowl for steaming (a large pasta bowl is often a good size for this job).

Using the bowl containing any remaining chermoula, add the lemon juice, honey, some sea salt and water, then mix. Pour the mixture over the fish and top with the preserved lemon rind.

Place the bowl containing the fish in the steamer or on the steamer tray and steam for 10–12 minutes. The timing will vary depending on the size of the fish pieces and the depth of the bowl the fish is sitting in. Test using a metal skewer or an unbent paper clip. Push the clip into the flesh, then put the clip against the skin below your lip. The fish is cooked if the clip feels warm.

Remove the steamer from the heat.

Carefully remove each portion of fish with a fish lifter and place in white bowls. Spoon the sauce left in the bowl over the fish. Sprinkle with the coriander leaves and serve immediately.

This is great served with couscous and a little steamed broccolini with garlic and chilli. If you like it really hot, add a dollop of harissa to the side.

NOTE: This recipe asks for preserved lemons which have to be stored for at least 6 weeks before they are ready to use, so if you haven't already made your preserved lemons you will have to buy them.

PRESERVED LEMONS

12 ripe lemons

1¾ cups (400g) sea salt

1 tablespoon coriander seeds

3 cinnamon sticks, crumbled

juice of 4–6 lemons

preserved lemons

Thoroughly wash the lemons in cold water to remove the waxy coating, then pat dry with paper towels.

Cut the lemons into quarters but not right the way through, leaving the last 1cm uncut.

Put 1 tablespoon of the sea salt in the middle of each lemon and close the lemon.

Take a large sterilised jar big enough to snugly fit the lemons and push the lemons well down into the jar, fitting as many as possible.

Intersperse the lemons with the coriander seeds and broken pieces of cinnamon.

Add the remaining salt and enough lemon juice to just cover. Make sure all the lemons are covered or they will not cure properly at the top and will go mouldy.

Seal the jar and put it in a cold dark place for at least 6 weeks.

HARISSA NO. 1

8 dried long red chillies, soaked overnight in water

1 teaspoon cumin seeds

1 teaspoon coriander seeds

4 cloves garlic, roughly chopped

1 teaspoon sea salt

⅓ cup (80ml) olive oil, plus extra

harissa no. 1

You will need to begin this recipe a day ahead.

makes about ½ cup

Remove the chillies from the water and reserve the water. Roughly chop the chillies. Remove the seeds if you want.

Roast the cumin and coriander seeds in a saucepan over heat until fragrant. Grind in a spice grinder or pound in a mortar to a fine powder. Put in a blender with the chilli, garlic, sea salt and oil and 2 tablespoons of the reserved water.

Blend to a rough paste, spoon into a sterilised jar and cover with a layer of oil.

HARISSA NO. 2

2 red capsicums, roasted and skinned (see page 56 for how to roast and skin capsicums)

2 teaspoons cumin seeds

½ teaspoon coriander seeds

2 cloves garlic peeled and roughly chopped

sea salt

¼ cup (60ml) extra virgin olive oil, plus extra

5 small red chillies, thinly sliced

HARISSA NO. 3

2 tablespoons fennel seeds

2 tablespoons cumin seeds

2 tablespoons coriander seeds

6 red capsicums, cut into strips

2 teaspoons sea salt

2 cups (500ml) extra virgin olive oil, plus extra

6 cloves garlic, sliced

70g palm sugar, grated

2 tablespoons fish sauce

1 tablespoon medium-strong chilli powder

juice of 2 lemons

harissa no. 2

makes about 1 cup

Heat the oven to 150°C (140°C fan forced).

Chop the capsicums, retaining the seeds.

Place the cumin and coriander in the oven and slow-roast for 10 minutes. Remove and allow to cool. Grind in a spice grinder or pound in a mortar to a fine powder.

Place the capsicum, capsicum seeds, ground spices, garlic and salt in a mortar and pound to a paste. Add 1 tablespoon of the oil, then add the chillies and pound to mix. Add the remaining oil and mix.

Spoon into a sterilised jar and cover with a layer of oil.

harissa no. 3

makes about 2 cups

Heat the oven to 150°C (140°C fan forced).

Slow-roast the fennel, cumin and coriander seeds in the oven for 10 minutes. Allow to cool, then grind in a spice grinder or pound in a mortar to a fine powder.

Put the capsicum, salt and oil in a large frying pan and cook over low heat for 1½–2 hours, then add the garlic and cook a further 2 minutes. Add the palm sugar, fish sauce, chilli and ground spices. Simmer for 5 minutes, then blitz in a food processor until smooth.

Add the lemon juice. Spoon into a sterilised jar and cover with a layer of oil.

— *neil perry*

Neil Perry

Neil Perry has taught me so much, dare I say it, about cooking Chinese food. We joked 'the round eye teaches the slant eye – how did this happen?' (Only I'm allowed to say that!) He's disarmingly calm, always, and it's this and his unfailing reputation as a businessman and world-class chef that might lead some people to think he's steely, cool and impenetrable, but in fact he's warm, cheeky and incredibly generous with his time and advice. I think everyone knows of the indelible mark he has made on the Australian food industry. But on a personal level Neil has taught me to think logically through cooking processes that I've always found very intimidating, like deep frying a whole duck. I just love that Neil cooks real, unapologetic Chinese that panders to no clichés. When I saw century egg on his restaurant menu, I knew we were friends in the making.

FUN FACTS:

• Neil comes from a family of butchers.

• Neil's love of Chinese food came from his father, a butcher, who loved taking young Neil to Sydney's Chinatown and introducing him to exotic ingredients like bitter melon.

• Neil trained as a hairdresser before discovering cooking.

Neil very generously invited me to cook with him at his home. That day we barbecued against a backdrop of the most stunning view of Sydney Harbour. I made traditional Malaysian satay while Neil taught me a few things about dry-aged beef.

In this episode I'd just made my yuba beads with Chinese pickles and Neil his three shot chicken.

eggplant and salted mackerel hotpot

½ cup (125ml) vegetable oil

1 x 80g salted mackerel cutlet (available from Asian grocers, vacuum packed or bottled in oil)

3 cloves garlic, thinly sliced

2 tablespoons finely shredded ginger

230g pork mince

100g prawns, minced or finely chopped

5-6 largish dried shiitake mushrooms, rehydrated in boiling water for 20 minutes, stems removed, squeezed and sliced (reserve liquid)

1 large (700g) eggplant, cut into 2 x 6cm thick batons

¼ teaspoon sesame oil

1 tablespoon shaoxing rice wine

1 tablespoon rice wine vinegar

1 tablespoon oyster sauce

2 cups (500ml) unsalted chicken stock (see page 49) or shiitake liquid or water

1 teaspoon sugar

2-3 spring onions, cut into 3cm batons

1 teaspoon cornflour

1 teaspoon chilli oil

coriander leaves, to garnish

steamed jasmine rice, to serve

This is most certainly my favourite hotpot dish. It features salted mackerel, which is a fantastic ingredient. When I was a tot, my great aunt used to give it to me crumbled over rice sitting in hot water as a snack, which I loved. If you can't be bothered traipsing around an Asian grocer, you can substitute with 6–7 large Italian anchovy fillets which I've done when I'm desperate. Although the flavour achieved is quite different, it does do the job by providing some depth to the salty characteristic required for the dish, which, like many Italian dishes that use anchovy, is not necessarily about the fish flavour being very prevalent.

serves 4

In a small frying pan or wok, heat 3 tablespoons of the oil over medium heat and shallow fry the mackerel until golden and crisp. The cutlet sometimes will fall apart when you are removing it from the oil. Don't worry. Drain the mackerel on paper towel, remove and discard bones and dark meat, and set aside. Only use 40g of the mackerel, otherwise your dish will end up too salty. As the fish is cured, it will last for weeks in an airtight container in the fridge.

Clean the wok completely or use a large saucepan. Heat the remaining 3 tablespoons of oil over medium-high heat. Lightly sauté the garlic and ginger until pale golden. Add the pork mince. Stir-fry until cooked. Add the prawn mince and mushrooms, and stir-fry for about 30 seconds. Add the eggplant and stir-fry for 30 seconds. Finely crumble the fried mackerel into the mixture. Add the sesame oil, the shaoxing, rice wine vinegar, oyster sauce, chicken stock or shiitake liquid or water. Cover and leave to braise for 10 minutes, or until the eggplant is tender. Stir in the sugar and spring onions.

Ladle 2 tablespoons of the sauce into a small mixing bowl, add the cornflour and stir until there are no lumps. Make a well in the middle of the wok by stirring continuously, pour the cornflour mixture into the well and stir until it boils and thickens considerably. Stir so the cornflour mixture is evenly distributed. Cook for another 30 seconds and season with more of the mackerel, if required.

Drizzle with the chilli oil and garnish with the coriander. Serve with steamed jasmine rice.

steamed egg custard with prawns and shiitake

160g peeled uncooked prawn flesh, chopped

2 teaspoons shaoxing rice wine

pinch of white pepper

1/2 teaspoon sugar

1 teaspoon soy sauce

4 large or 12 small shiitake mushrooms, soaked in hot water for 20 minutes, drained and squeezed

4 large free-range eggs

1¼ cups (310ml) chicken stock (page 49)

pinch of salt and white pepper

Topping

1 spring onion, finely chopped

2 teaspoons light soy sauce

1½ tablespoons peanut or vegetable oil with a few drops of sesame oil mixed in

I absolutely adore this dish and strangely it's one I always forget to pull out of the hat considering it's delicious and so quick to make. Both the Japanese and the Chinese do a version of this. In Japan, it's called chawanmushi, which means 'steamed in a tea cup' and in China, it's referred to as 'soi tan', which means 'watery egg'. The texture is divinely silky and you can steam it with any seafood you like. My sister in law, Teena, does a fantastic version with century and salted duck eggs, which my little nephews go crazy over.

serves 4

Half fill a wok with water, place a large bamboo steamer on top. Ensure the steamer will hold 4 Chinese rice bowls or ramekins around 25cm in diameter comfortably.

Combine the chopped prawns, shaoxing, pepper, sugar and soy sauce and set aside to marinate for 10 minutes.

Remove and discard the woody stems of the shiitake and slice. Set aside.

In a bowl, briefly mix the eggs, stock and salt and pepper. Using a pair of chopsticks do slow figure 8s to do the mixing, rather than madly whisking, you will achieve a much silkier result.

Divide the prawns, mushrooms and egg mixture into the 4 bowls and steam with the bamboo lid on for 7–10 minutes. The custards should be an opaque creamy colour when done and still very wobbly.

Remove the bowls from the steamer, sprinkle each one with the chopped spring onion and ½ teaspoon of the soy sauce. Heat the peanut oil in a small saucepan, until beginning to smoke. Immediately pour over each egg custard but be careful, there will be some spitting. Serve while hot.

prawn and yuba beads

500g uncooked peeled prawn flesh, chopped

250g pork mince

1½ teaspoons cornflour

1 teaspoon sugar

1 teaspoon salt

1½ teaspoons white pepper

1 large free-range egg

5 large shiitake mushrooms, soaked in hot water 20–30 minutes, stalks discarded, squeezed and chopped finely

1 tablespoon shaoxing rice wine

150g water chestnuts, cut into matchsticks

250g Chinese soft bean curd skins (not the pale yellow brittle sort; but the flexible golden colour and translucent ones)

4 cups (1 litre) vegetable or peanut oil

Thai-style chilli oil

CHINESE PICKLES

1⅓ cups (300g) sugar

1 cup white vinegar

3 medium carrots, peeled, cut into 3cm long matchsticks

20 radishes, unpeeled, scrubbed, cut in half and sliced thinly

1½ continental cucumbers, unpeeled cut into quarters lengthways, seeds sliced off, thinly sliced diagonally

1¼ teaspoons salt

This is an old family dish that I'd long forgotten. It uses some interesting cooking techniques that the Chinese are very fond of, steaming and then deep-frying, which is a great way to ensure you don't find yourself frying the outside of a parcel to golden perfection, while nervously wondering whether the inside is cooked. For this dish, you will need kitchen string and a bamboo basket.

makes 40–50 rolls, serves 8–10 as an entree

Mix all the ingredients together except for the bean curd skins, vegetable and chilli oil. Work the mixture with your hands until it is very sticky and opaque.

Lay out one bean curd skin and smooth it out. Starting 3cm in from the left edge, spoon some of the prawn and pork mixture onto the skin in a long thin line so when it is rolled up it is about the thickness of a regular sausage. Leave a 5cm space at the other end. Roll up the skin, making sure the mixture is tucked in well with no cavities. Roll the sausage about 4 rotations. With kitchen string, start by tying and knotting from the left, making small balls along the sausage, so it resembles a chain of beads. You should be able to fit 7–8 beads per sausage, if not your sausage has too much stuffing. Repeat until all the bean curd skins are used. Place the chains in a dish or bamboo steamer (they can lie close to one another) and steam for 10 minutes.

In a wok, heat the vegetable or peanut oil over medium heat and deep-fry the beads until golden. Drain on paper towel. When cool, cut and remove the string at the tied intervals. You may return the beads to the wok to crispen where the beads were tied, drain on a paper towel once more, then serve with a sprinkle of chilli oil on top and the Chinese pickles.

Chinese pickles

Heat the sugar and vinegar until the sugar dissolves. Cool.

Combine the vegetables, sprinkle on the salt and gently toss with your hands. Sit in a colander in the fridge for 3 hours.

Gently squeeze out excess liquid, pour on the vinegar mixture and refrigerate in a glass jar for at least 1 day before eating.

paella

1 large pinch of saffron strands

2 tablespoons extra virgin olive oil

250g chorizo or other spicy sausage, cut into bite size pieces

500g skinless chicken thigh fillets, cut into 2–3cm pieces

1 large onion, chopped

2 capsicums (1 red, 1 green or yellow), cut into strips

2 cloves garlic, chopped

1 cup (150g) cherry tomatoes, cut in half

2–3 teaspoons smoked paprika (or ordinary paprika)

1 bay leaf

3 cups (640g) medium-grain rice

4 cups (1 litre) chicken stock (see page 49), approximately

12 (approximately 300g) green prawns in shells

12 (approximately 300g) mussels

400g white fish fillets, cut into bite size pieces

1 cup (155g) frozen peas (optional)

One of the world's classic rice dishes from Spain – a fabulous mixture of rice, chicken, seafood, vegetables and saffron. A tasty, visual treat that is fun to prepare, its name comes not from the dish itself but from the pan it is cooked in, a sort of two-handled frying pan. However, any large frying pan with a capacity of about 3 litres – or an electric frying pan – will do. I usually make enough for about 10 people. There is no absolutely right or wrong way to make paella … there are so many versions, depending on the region it comes from. This version has no claim to being Spanish and is often cooked over an open fire.

serves 10–12

Immerse the saffron in 2 tablespoons of boiling water for 5 minutes.

Heat the oil in a large frying pan over medium heat and partly cook the chorizo for a few minutes. Add the chicken and cook for 3–4 minutes, or until browned. It doesn't need to be cooked right through at this stage. Add the onion, capsicum, garlic, cherry tomatoes, paprika and bay leaf and cook for 2-3 minutes.

Add the rice and stir for a couple of minutes. Pour in the stock and the saffron liquid (discard the saffron strands) and add enough water to cover the rice by 1cm. Cover with foil, reduce the heat to low and simmer for 15 minutes, or until the liquid is almost absorbed.

Meanwhile, rinse and drain the prawns in cold water. Scrub and de-beard the mussels in cold water, and discard any that have opened or are cracked.

Dot the prawns, mussels and fish over the rice mixture. The frozen peas may be added at this time. Cook for a further 10 minutes, or until the seafood is just cooked. Discard any mussels that have not opened.

— *Ian Parmenter*

Ian Parmenter

Ian Parmenter is pure joy to be around. The funny thing is that the off-the-wall character you see on TV is pretty much Ian being utterly himself. On entering a room, he always throws his arms out, quite theatrically announcing 'hello', and instantly everyone feels warmed. His try-everything attitude and genuine zest for life is something I completely identify with. He's also a proud cook, not a chef, which we also have in common. For years I wanted to meet the madman from *Consuming Passions* who taught me how to cook ego noodles and instantly it was as if I'd known him for years – we are peas in a pod. His food is delicious and unpretentious, driven by the seasons of the beautiful Margaret River region. He is completely unbridled by social conventions and his kooky sense of humour is right up my alley.

FUN FACTS:

• With no access to a kitchen and lots of fresh seafood in his possession, Ian was once driven to cook scallops with an iron from a hotel room — sorry housekeeping!

• We are both mad about noodles.

• Before falling in love with Margaret River, Ian was 'deeply suspicious' of the country.

Ian was a wonderful host while I was visiting the very bottom left-hand corner of Australia. Here we had just cooked his paella at the local farmer's market and visited a beautiful school-kitchen garden.

marron with roasted salad and grapefruit dressing

The grapefruit is one of our newer fruits. Originating in the West Indies, it has only been around for a couple of hundred years, and is a cross between the orange and the pommelo, another large citrus fruit. My favourite variety is the pink fleshed ruby grapefruit, which was discovered in Texas in the late 1920s. The dressing works really well in this salad with the native crustacean of Margaret River, marron. Lobster or other shellfish could be used.

serves 1

Salad

1–2 small zucchini

1 small eggplant

extra virgin olive oil

2 teaspoons grated lemon zest

sea salt

freshly ground black pepper

1 large marron (see note below)

6–7 small tomatoes, halved

several basil leaves, shredded

SALAD

Slice the zucchini and eggplant lengthways. Score the flesh with a knife in a criss-cross fashion. Place on a baking tray lined with baking paper and brush with a little olive oil mixed with the lemon zest. Season with salt and pepper. Bake until cooked, 10–15 minutes depending on the size of the pieces.

Place the marron on a baking tray, brush the flesh with the olive oil, sprinkle with salt and pepper. Bake for 6–8 minutes, or until cooked (the flesh should feel firm). Allow the marron and vegetables to cool a little before serving.

Put the eggplant and zucchini on a serving plate, then top with the marron, tomatoes and basil, and pour on the grapefruit dressing.

Dressing (makes 1 cup)

2 ruby grapefruit (or other variety but ruby are best)

½ cup (125ml) extra virgin olive oil

2 teaspoons honey (I use red gum or leatherwood)

1 large rosemary sprig, leaves picked, chopped

2 teaspoons horseradish sauce

freshly ground black pepper

DRESSING

Cut the top and bottom off 1 grapefruit and peel by cutting down right through to the flesh, cutting away the rind, pith and skin, following the line of the fruit. Then cut out the individual segments.

In a bowl, mix the juice of the remaining grapefruit with the olive oil, honey, rosemary, horseradish sauce and black pepper. Mix well and stir in the grapefruit segments.

This beautiful, fruity salad dressing works particularly well with smoked fish.

....

NOTE: If the marron is alive, chill in the freezer to put it to sleep. Then slice lengthways and clean.

....

— *Ian Parmenter*

poultry
and meat

crispy taro-crusted duck with Mandarin sauce

1 x 2kg pekin duck (see note)

peanut oil, for frying

Marinade

1½ tablespoons light soy sauce

¼ cup (60ml) shaoxing rice wine

2 spring onions, white part only, cut into rounds

2 pieces dried orange peel

3cm knob ginger, peeled and finely diced

1 star anise, crushed

20g yellow rock sugar

Coating

2 egg whites

¼ cup (50g) taro flour

2 tablespoons rice flour

Mandarin sauce

100g palm sugar, grated

peel from 2 mandarins, cut into matchsticks

3 tablespoons ginger, cut into matchsticks

2½ tablespoons fish sauce

2½ tablespoons fresh mandarin juice

2 mandarins, segmented

Begin this recipe the day before you plan to eat it.

serves 4

Place the duck on a chopping board and remove the fat from the cavity. Cut off the wings and neck, and with a cleaver split the duck in half.

Boil the marinade ingredients together for 2 minutes. Allow to cool and rub the marinade all over the duck. Marinate for 3 hours, or preferably overnight.

Place the duck in a steamer and steam for 45 minutes. Remove from the heat and set aside until cool enough to handle. Carefully remove the bones, taking care not to break the skin. Use a small knife to ease out the wing and leg bones. Deboning is easier when the duck is slightly warm as it presses together much better. At the end of this step you should have 2 rectangles of duck. Place them on a board and fold all the skin under the duck. Cover the pieces loosely with clingfilm (allow some slack so they can spread). Put them in a container and place another container that fits inside the first on top, then a 5kg weight. Refrigerate overnight.

Take the ducks out of the container and unwrap. You should have 2 solid pieces of duck with flat smooth skin. Place a steamer on the stove over some boiling water.

To coat the duck, whisk the egg whites in a bowl until they start to thicken, but before soft peaks form. Mix the two flours together. Dip the duck into the egg white, skinside down. Ensure there is an even covering of egg white over the skin. With a sieve, dust the duck with the two flours, blow off any excess and place on a heatproof plate.

Place both pieces of duck in the steamer and cook for 20–25 minutes. The egg white crust should be dry to the touch, if it is undercooked it will detach from the duck during the later frying process, so ensure that it is cooked through.

NOTE: Pekin ducks are a breed that originally came from Nanjing, China. Not to be confused with Peking duck, which is a famous duck dish from Beijing.

To make the mandarin sauce, place the palm sugar with a little water in a saucepan and bring to the boil. Add the mandarin peel and ginger and continue to cook until a dark caramel colour. Add the fish sauce and mandarin juice and stir. Add the mandarin segments and set aside, keep warm.

Add enough peanut oil to a wok (or deep-fryer) to submerge the duck pieces, and heat to 180°C. Add the duck pieces and fry for 6 minutes, or until the coating is crisp and the duck is warmed through. Remove and drain. Rest in a warm place.

To serve, cut the duck pieces into finger wide slices and spoon the sauce over the top. This is fantastic served with stir-fried spinach.

— Neil Perry

In Tasmania, in one of Matt Marston's wasabi patches, were these absolute cuties. Matt's little girl informed me that these pekin ducks were actually hatched by a broody hen.

crispy-skinned 5-spice duck with Mandarin pancakes

Mandarin pancakes (makes about 14)

220g plain flour

½ teaspoon salt

150–170ml boiling water

sesame oil for basting

extra flour for dusting

Peking Duck is something my family almost always orders when we dine out and are eating Chinese. Traditional Peking duck is quite an involved process and impossible to replicate at home, so I've come up with this solution, which isn't Peking Duck at all but it will satisfy any PD craving. You can use chicken or quail (but skip the pancakes), and serve with any leftover spice salt steeped in 2–3 tablespoons of fresh lemon juice as a dipping sauce which is also delicious.

serves 6

MANDARIN PANCAKES

In a medium bowl, mix the flour, salt and water roughly with a fork until the ingredients start to come together. Then scrunch the mixture together with your hands. At first it will be hot, so you'll need to do it in quick bursts, but as it cools you'll be able to handle the dough with ease. When most of the dough is gathered into a mass, tip it onto the bench and knead until relatively smooth, adding a little more water or flour if required. Rest the dough under a damp tea towel for 30 minutes.

Knead the dough for a further few minutes until it is smooth and not sticky. Divide the dough into half and roll each half into a cylinder about 4cm in diameter. Divide each cylinder into 7 discs. Lightly flour them and squash them down with the palm of your hand, making sure they keep their circular shape. With a pastry brush, brush a liberal amount of sesame oil on one disk and then place another disk on top. Pair all the disks together like this and place them under a tea towel to keep from drying out. Roll out each paired disc to about 2mm thick and 10–12cm in diameter.

Heat a frying pan to medium-high heat and dry panfry the pancakes on both sides until dark brown dots appear on the surface. Remove from the frying pan and immediately find the seam where the 2 disks meet and carefully peel the 2 pancakes apart making sure that the steam trapped between them doesn't burn you. Fold each pancake in half, and rest under a damp tea towel before serving. These actually store in the fridge or freezer very well but you will need to steam them before eating. Even when freshly made, you may want to steam for a few minutes in a bamboo basket to refresh and warm them before serving with the duck.

2 x 250g duck breasts, with skin on

700ml peanut or vegetable oil

⅓ cup (40g) cornflour for dusting

⅓-½ cup (80-125ml) hoisin sauce

⅓ of a continental cucumber, peeled, quartered lengthways, seeds sliced out, and cut into 7cm batons

2 spring onions, 7cm of white part only, cut into matchsticks lengthways

Spice salt

1 tablespoon salt

1 teaspoon 5-spice powder

2 teaspoons Szechuan pepper

Marinade

1 teaspoon shaoxing rice wine

1 teaspoon light soy sauce

¼ teaspoon sugar

pinch of white pepper

2 x 5mm slices of ginger bashed with the palm of your hand

1 spring onion snapped in half and twisted up

To make the spice salt, toast all the ingredients in a small frying pan until fragrant and beginning to smoke. Set aside.

Mix all the marinade ingredients together in a bowl.

Score the duck skin with 2-3 mm paralle slits, then repeat in a perpendicular direction to create a lattice effect. Do not cut right through. To be perfectly honest, if you can't be bothered scoring the skin, the result isn't hugely affected, but it's nice to go the extra mile. Rub just enough spice salt over the duck to coat it. You will have some left over. Transfer to a plate with some depth to it and pour over the marinade. Cover with clingfilm and refrigerate for 1-3 hours.

Place a cake cooling rack or metal trivet in a wok. Fill the wok with enough warm water to reach about 2cm below the rack. Place the plate of duck on the rack. Heat the water to boiling and steam the duck for 5 minutes, covered.

Meanwhile, using a cooking thermometer, heat the oil in another wok to about 160-170°C.

Transfer the duck onto a chopping board, pat thoroughly dry with a paper towel to remove all excess moisture (otherwise it will spit ferociously when you deep fry it). Coat the duck pieces in the cornflour, shaking off any excess, and deep fry for about 6-7 minutes. Rest for 5 minutes and then carve into diagonal slices about 5mm thick.

To serve, open the pancake and smear a teaspoon of the hoisin sauce on it, then place a few pieces of duck, one baton of cucumber and a few slivers of spring onion and roll up into a long parcel. Don't waste the delicious duck juices from the steaming - reserve and eat it mixed into a small bowl of rice.

three-shot chicken

5 small dried shiitake mushrooms

2 cups (500ml) chicken stock plus
  2 tablespoons extra

8 cloves garlic, peeled

1–2 tablespoons peanut oil

250g skinless chicken thigh fillets,
  cut into 2cm cubes

½ carrot peeled, cut into rounds

2 tablespoons sweet bean paste

2cm piece (15g) peeled ginger, cut
  into matchsticks

1½ tablespoons shaoxing rice wine

1 large shot (60ml) each light soy
  sauce, beer and chilli oil

steamed jasmine rice, to serve

For this recipe, you need a seasoned clay pot. If you are going to finish the dish with the shots at the table, you will also need a small portable burner.

serves 4 as part of a shared meal

Soak the mushrooms in hot water for 1 hour, or until softened. Cut off the hard stems and discard. Bring the chicken stock to a simmer and braise the mushrooms and garlic for 15 minutes, or until soft. The garlic will take less time, so remove it first if you need to continue cooking the mushrooms. Remove the garlic and mushrooms from the stock and set aside.

Add a little of the peanut oil to a hot wok and stir-fry the chicken over high heat for 2–3 minutes, or until golden. Remove the chicken from the wok and set aside with the mushrooms and garlic.

Add more oil if needed, stir-fry the bean paste for 1 minute, then add the ginger, deglaze with the shaoxing, then add the extra chicken stock. Return the chicken, mushrooms and garlic, add the carrots to the wok and combine with the sauce.

Pour the entire contents into a clay pot and light the fire and heat to a good simmer. Add the shots and cook for 3–5 minutes. Serve with rice.

— neil perry

twice-cooked salt pork with black beans and Chinese leek

20 cups (5 litres) of water

250g salt

1.5cm piece (10g) ginger, peeled and sliced

2 cloves garlic, peeled and sliced

5 eschalot ends

100g yellow rock sugar

1kg whole pork belly, bones removed

2½ tablespoons peanut oil

1 Chinese leek, trimmed and cut into 1cm lengths

1.5cm piece (10g) peeled ginger, smashed

1 clove garlic, peeled and smashed

1 tablespoon fermented black beans

6 stems garlic chives, cut into 3cm lengths

8 stems garlic shoots, cut into 3cm lengths

6 spring onions, cut into 3cm lengths

pinch of sea salt

2 tablespoons shaoxing rice wine

1 tablespoon chicken stock

serves 4 as part of a shared meal

To salt-braise the white pork belly, bring the first 6 ingredients to the boil in a large saucepan.

Add the pork belly, reduce the heat to low and braise the pork slowly for 2 hours, or until very tender. Remove the pan from the heat and allow the pork to cool in the stock.

When cool, remove the pork from the stock and refrigerate until ready to use. (See note below).

Slice the salt-braised white pork belly into 1cm thick slices.

Place the peanut oil in a wok and stir-fry the white pork belly slices until golden. Remove.

Fry the Chinese leek until golden. Remove and set aside.

Fry the ginger and garlic until fragrant then add the black beans, garlic chives, garlic shoots and spring onions along with the salt.

Deglaze with the shaoxing. Add the stock, then return the pork and leek to the wok and combine.

Serve straightaway.

— *Neil Perry*

NOTE: Strain the stock and refrigerate or freeze. It can be re-used in any braised pork recipe.

dong do pork

1kg pork belly

3 tablespoons peanut or vegetable oil to fry

4 spring onions, sliced

10 slices ginger, each about 4mm thick

125g yellow rock sugar

3½ tablespoons dark soy sauce

3½ tablespoons light soy sauce

150ml shaoxing rice wine

½ cup (125ml) water

If you enjoy a store-bought char siew (Chinese barbecue pork), this is a far superior homemade version. During the cooking process it develops the most beautiful glossy mahogany colour all over, and the meat on the inside melts in your mouth. One of the best memories I have of this dish, apart from it being absolutely delicious, was after cooking this for the first time with my Great Auntie Kim. I was about to dump the cooking pot into the sink after we'd dished the pork and sauce out. She stopped me in my tracks, made me put the pot down while she returned from the fridge with a bowl of leftover rice. She tipped the rice into the pot, swished all the grains around with her hand to mop up all that beautiful caramalisation, scooped it back into the bowl, covered it and said in Cantonese, 'lunch tomorrow', then briskly walked away to tend to some gardening … she's brilliant like that, my auntie …

serves 5-6 as part of a shared meal

To prepare the pork belly, score the skin with 5mm parallel slits, then repeat in a perpendicular direction to create a lattice effect. This will help to render off some of the top layer of fat during cooking.

Heat the oil in a wok over medium heat. First place the pork with the skin side down, to render some of the fat and crisp it up (this takes about 5 minutes) before browning all sides. I do suggest wearing oven mitts at the stage to turn the meat. Moisture will be leaching out of the meat as it caramelises, so there can be a bit of dramatic spitting. Set aside when all sides have been sealed (takes about 4-5 minutes each side) and have developed some good colour.

Combine the spring onions, ginger, sugar, both soy sauces, wine and water in a heavy-based non-stick saucepan over medium heat until the sugar dissolves. Lower the pork into the saucepan and simmer for 2-2½ hours (turning the meat a few times during the cooking process), or until the meat is very tender. If necessary, add 1-2 tablespoons of water to prevent the sauce from burning and sticking to the bottom. The sauce should be a sticky glaze. Rest for 15 minutes.

Cut the pork into long thin slices, like bacon, and serve as a sharing dish with rice and some steamed Asian greens.

slow roasted rib of beef

2- or 3-bone rib of beef (2–3 ribs will be enough for 4 people), preferably dry-aged for at least 3 weeks

sea salt

extra virgin olive oil

freshly ground black pepper

serves 4

Preheat the oven to 75°C, or as low as it will go.

Take the rib out of the refrigerator 2 hours before you intend to cook it and season it well with salt. Let it come to room temperature. (Alternatively, you can season it the night before.) Rub the rib with the oil and put in a large roasting tin. Place in the oven and turn the dish every 30 minutes or so. After 1½ hours, slide the meat thermometer into the centre of the beef to check the core temperature, remove the thermometer and continue to cook until the core reaches 53°C. This will take between 3 and 4 hours. Remember that if your oven is a little hotter, you will need to take the meat out when it is a degree or two lower. (See note below.)

When the meat is done, put it on a chopping board. Carefully remove the bones from the beef (alternatively, you can leave the meat on the bone, sear it and serve on the bone). Turn the oven down as low as it will go (you may need to leave the door slightly ajar), as you want to create a warm environment of around 60°C in which to rest the meat.

In a frying pan large enough to hold the beef, add a healthy splash of the oil and heat on the stove to just below smoking. Add the beef and sear, turning 3cm at a time, until the entire rib has a lovely crust. Return to the roasting tin and put in the oven for 30 minutes to rest while you get the other parts of the meal together, or at least get your guests a drink.

On a chopping board, cut the rib into four beautiful rose-red round slices and place one each in the centre of four plates. Drizzle with the oil and season liberally with pepper. Serve immediately with accompaniments.

I like to serve it with spinach puree, potato gratin and horseradish cream, or a little red wine sauce – only a tablespoon, more will overpower the beef.

NOTE: You have a meat thermometer, so you can cook the meat at whatever temperature you like, but if you cook it at a high temperature – say at around 200°C – you will have to take it out when its internal temperature is 48–49°C, as the meat's core temperature will continue to rise a fair bit due to the residual cooking. The meat will also benefit from a much longer resting period, about 1 hour. You won't need to seal the beef, however, as the high heat will do that for you.

POTATO GRATIN

500g bintje (yellow finn) or other waxy potatoes

1 cup (250ml) pouring cream

sea salt and freshly ground pepper

20g unsalted butter, melted

potato gratin

serves 4-6

Peel and cut the potatoes into 2mm thick slices, covering the slices with the cream to prevent discolouration. Season the potato slices with sea salt and freshly ground pepper. Brush the base and sides of a shallow baking tray or gratin dish with the melted butter. Remove the potato slices from the cream and overlap them in lines down the dish until about 2–3 cm deep. If using a round dish, arrange the slices in a circle and cover the middle with another circle of potato. Drizzle a little cream between each layer. Pour any remaining cream over. Bake at 190°C (180°C fan forced) for 50–60 minutes, or until lightly browned and tender.

RED WINE SAUCE

olive oil

1 small carrot, peeled and finely diced

½ red onion, finely diced

2 cloves garlic, chopped

2 field mushrooms, chopped

150g meat trimmings, chopped

100ml balsamic vinegar

1½ tablespoons red wine vinegar

150ml port

2 cups (500ml) full bodied red wine

2 thyme sprigs

½ cup (125ml) veal stock, optional

knob of butter, to finish

red wine sauce

makes about 150ml

Make this red wine reduction with a good quality, full bodied red wine; don't use wine that is not pleasant to drink or you will end up with something that is not rich enough. Cook the reduction with some meat scraps, bacon or pancetta as they add flavour and help remove any bitter and sour flavours from the wine.

Put a little olive oil in a small saucepan and add the carrot, onion, garlic, mushrooms and meat trimmings. Cook until lightly coloured and the meat is well sealed. Add the vinegars and reduce to barely 2½ tablespoons. Add the port and again reduce to barely 2½ tablespoons. Add the red wine and thyme and reduce to 150ml, then strain.

You can add veal stock and reduce further. When it is ready to serve, whisk in a little butter. Alternatively, leave out the stock and only add the butter for a rich butter sauce.

— Neil Perry

Richard Nicholl's poll herefords at Cape Grim, Tasmania. These guys will sometimes venture on to the beach and help themselves to kelp for a dose of sea minerals.

rabbit in white wine or beer

1 rabbit, jointed

3 tablespoons Dijon mustard

3 teaspoons olive oil

60g unsalted butter

200g speck, diced

8 red eschalots, finely chopped

2 cloves garlic, finely chopped

400g button mushrooms or 1 can

1/2 cup (60g) plain flour for dusting

bouquet garni (4 sprigs of parsley
and thyme and 2 bay leaves,
tied together)

800ml chicken stock (see page 49)

1 cup (250ml) dry white wine or
330 ml bottle of beer

10 baby new potatoes, peeled,
halved and par-boiled

10 thyme sprigs

100ml pouring cream (optional)

salt to taste

1/4 teaspoon freshly cracked pepper

Glazed carrots

1 bunch baby carrots

50g unsalted butter

1/2 teaspoon salt

1/2 cup (125ml) water

1 teaspoon sugar

3 tablespoons chopped flat leaf
parsley, to garnish

I only became acquainted with rabbit about a year ago. Initially, a little squeamish about eating Thumper, I now love its subtle, earthy characteristics. Do take note of the concept of caramelising each ingredient before it goes into the oven. These are the building blocks which will make for a beautiful, richly flavoured stew.

serves 4

With a pastry brush, thoroughly brush the rabbit pieces with the mustard. Season with salt and pepper. Heat the oil and 25g of the butter in a heavy-based casserole dish and allow to become very hot. Add the rabbit pieces in batches of 3–4, taking care not to overcrowd the dish, and seal. Brown every piece for 2–3 minutes on all sides. Remove and set aside.

Preheat oven to 180°C (170°C fan forced).

Melt the remaining butter with the speck in the same pan, add the eschalots and brown, then add the garlic and sauté until aromatic but not brown. Add the mushrooms and sauté until slightly caramelised. Remove from heat.

Dust each piece of rabbit with the flour and return to the dish. Add the bouquet garni and pour the stock and wine or beer over the rabbit, return to the heat and bring to the boil. Add the potatoes and thyme. Place in the oven and cook for 1–1½ hours, or until the rabbit is falling off the bone.

Stir in the cream (if using) and season with salt and pepper. Cover and set aside.

GLAZED CARROTS

Cut the green tops off the carrots leaving 1cm still attached and peel. In a saucepan, melt 25g of the butter with the salt, water and sugar. Add the carrots and simmer for 10-15 minutes, or until nearly all the liquid has evaporated and the carrots are just tender. If the water has evaporated before the carrots have cooked, add ¼ cup of water. Dollop the last of the butter on top, and shake the pan so the carrots are coated with a nice gloss. Serve immediately, scattered over the top of the stew and garnish with the parsley.

lamb shank ragout with fettuccine

⅓ cup (80ml) olive oil

5 lamb shanks

3 medium brown onions, chopped

3 cloves garlic, finely chopped

1 bay leaf

1 large carrot, finely chopped

1 stick celery, finely chopped

30g dried porcini mushrooms, soaked in boiling water to rehydrate, drained (reserve liquid)

1 large red capsicum, char grilled, peeled and sliced into 4 x 1cm strips

10 medium tomatoes, peeled and chopped

½ cup (125ml) red wine

1½ cups (375ml) beef stock (see page 49)

1–2 teaspoon red wine vinegar (only if you think the end result needs more acid for balance)

1 x 500g packet of fettuccine or gnocchi (see page 155)

¼ cup chopped flat-leaf parsley

I first tasted a version of this dish at my friend Nat's house. I was feeling decidedly down at the time and the care she showed inviting me over for a beautiful home cooked meal and sincere friendship made the dish more than just delicious … food is love!

serves 4

Set oven to 180°C (170°C fan forced).

In a large frying pan, heat 3 tablespoons of the olive oil on medium-high heat to seal the shanks. Caramelise as much of the surface area of each shank as possible. Always remember, colour is flavour, so take the caramelisation as far as you can without charring. Set aside.

Pour the excess oil from sealing the shanks and the remaining olive oil into a heavy based casserole pot but do not wash the frying pan. Heat the pot to medium heat and sauté the onions, garlic and bay leaf until fragrant but not coloured. Add the carrot and celery, and sauté until both are tender. Add the porcini and sauté for a few seconds. Add the shanks, capsicum and chopped tomatoes to the pot and bring to the boil.

Meanwhile, return the frying pan to a medium heat and deglaze with the red wine and ½ of the beef stock. Simmer gently and with a wooden spoon loosen *all* the caramelisation on the bottom of the pan. Pour this liquid into the pot over the shanks, including the remaining beef stock. Bring to the boil once more, cover and cook in the oven for 1½–2 hours or until the shanks are tender.

When the ragout is close to being done, boil a large pot of water with a tablespoon of salt in it ready to cook the fettuccine. Alternatively, you can serve with gnocchi.

When the ragout is out of the oven, fish out all the shanks, and remove the flesh and shred into smaller pieces, discarding any gristly bits. At this point, taste and check for balance. If you think the sauce needs a little more acid, add the red wine vinegar. Return the flesh to the pot and reduce a little further if the sauce isn't very thick. As this reduces, cook the fettuccine *al dente* (Italian for 'to the tooth'), drain but do not rinse as this will stop the sauce from sticking to the pasta and lower the temperature too much. Add the sauce and toss. Serve with a garnish of chopped parsley.

roast leg of lamb with rosemary and garlic

1 x 2kg leg of lamb

2 tablespoons Dijon or seeded
    mustard

1 teaspoon salt

2 tablespoons olive oil

4-5 cloves garlic, sliced

7-8 rosemary sprigs, cut into
    2.5cm length

Gravy

1 teaspoon plain flour

1/2 cup (125ml) red wine

1/3 cup (80ml) water or 1/2 cup
    (125ml) beef stock (see page 49)

1 1/2 teaspoons sugar

1/2 teaspoon red wine vinegar

30g unsalted butter, diced

1/2 teaspoon salt, or to taste

freshly ground black pepper

I finally did it. I tackled a roast and it was remarkably easy, painless even. I even managed to get it perfectly medium, which I have to confess to being quite proud of. So there you have it, the Chinese girl eventually cooks a roast!

Heat the oven to 220°C (210°C fan forced).

In a small bowl mix the mustard, salt and oil. Massage all over the leg of lamb, then with a small paring knife make about 50 incisions which are 1.5cm wide and 2cm deep, all over the fleshy parts of the leg. In each slit stuff a slice of garlic then a stem of rosemary.

Place the leg on a large roasting tin, cover loosely with foil and roast in the oven for 15 minutes. Turn the oven down to 170°C (160°C fan forced), remove the foil and roast for a further 40-45 minutes for medium or 50-55 minutes for medium-well done. Remove from the oven, place on a plate, cover with foil and rest for 30-40 minutes before carving.

To make the gravy, place the roasting tin on the stovetop and bring the pan juices to the boil. Add the flour and mix with a fork or whisk until there are no lumps. Stir for a minute or until the flour is cooked. You will know it is ready when the flour begins to foam. Pour in the red wine and keep stirring until incorporated. Bring to the boil and reduce for 1 minute before adding water or stock, sugar and red wine vinegar. Bring back to the boil. Finally, whisk in the butter for a nice glossy finish. Adjust seasoning if required and add pepper.

Carve the lamb and serve with the gravy, perfect carrots, braised red cabbage, caramelised sweet corn, witlof and smashed potatoes, all of which are on pages 104-105.

hot vegetable sides

I do love the homogenous mass of pure comfort that roast veggies provide but at the same time, avoiding your usual suspects is a good way to modernise the roast by giving each vegetable some individual attention, and when you're short for time, it's perfectly good to do just one or two, well. The other advantage to all these vegetable sides is that most of them are done on the stovetop which means it's much easier to maintain the balancing act of all the accompaniments to the roast landing on the dinner table hot.

each recipe serves 4

CARAMELISED WITLOF AND SWEET CORN

25g unsalted butter

4 heads of witlof, quartered lengthways

½ cup (60g) pure icing sugar for dusting

1 head of corn, kernels sliced off

juice ¼–½ orange

caramelised witlof and sweet corn

Melt the butter in a large non-stick frying pan until it begins to foam. Dust the witlof in icing sugar and toss in the pan with the corn. Cook for about 7 minutes, or until the witlof and corn are caramelised with a few golden edges. Deglaze the pan with the orange juice to lift off the caramelised bits, and season with salt and pepper.

BRAISED RED CABBAGE

500g red cabbage, central stalk discarded, finely shredded

50g unsalted butter

¼ cup (125ml) apple cider vinegar

¾ cup (80ml) water

1 teaspoon sugar

½ teaspoon salt

freshly ground black pepper

braised red cabbage

Combine all the ingredients in a saucepan and braise for 10–15 minutes. Only about 1–2 tablespoons of liquid should remain and the cabbage should be tender but still have a bite to it. Season further if required.

PERFECT CARROTS

1 bunch baby carrots, peeled or scraped

1 teaspoon sugar

½ cup (125ml) water

½ teaspoon salt

25g unsalted butter

1 tablespoon chopped flat leaf parsley

SMASHED POTATOES

6–7 medium desiree potatoes, peeled

generous drizzle olive oil

2 teaspoons thyme or rosemary leaves, chopped

125g butter or duck or goose fat

sea salt flakes and freshly cracked black pepper

perfect carrots

Combine the carrots, sugar, water and salt in a small saucepan and simmer until the carrots are just tender and nearly all the water has evaporated. If the carrots are not cooked enough, add a few tablespoons of water and simmer until tender. Toss in butter and allow this to melt and coat the carrots so there is a beautiful gloss. Serve with a sprinkle of parsley over the top.

smashed potatoes

Don't be concerned about the amount of potatoes, which seems a lot for 4, but they do shrink a lot in the oven.

Heat the oven to 200°C (190°C fan forced).

In a large saucepan of water, boil the potatoes until just tender. Drain and allow to cool a little. Then with the palm of your hand, press down on each potato so it crumbles and falls apart. Make sure you split any pieces that are too chunky, so they are about the size of a large cherry.

Line a baking tray with baking paper and drizzle generously with olive oil. Place the potato chunks onto the tray and sprinkle the thyme or rosemary and small chunks of butter or duck fat over the potatoes and place in oven. Roast for 35–40 minutes, or until all the little nuggets are as golden brown as can be without being burnt. Occasionally take the tray out of the oven to shake and coat the potatoes with the fat or butter. Season with the salt and pepper and serve.

TIP: I always pare the ends of baby carrots down to make perfectly pointy tips, as it makes for gorgeous presentation which guests always notice. Also make sure the bit where the green top sprouts from is scrubbed or scaped clean.

stuffed lamb cutlets

8 large young lamb cutlets, trimmed of fat

2 slices prosciutto cut into quarters

8 sage leaves

8 small slices fontina or Gruyere cheese

2 eggs, beaten with salt and pepper

about 6 tablespoons dried white breadcrumbs, to coat

olive oil, for shallow-frying

serves 4

With a sharp pointed knife, make an incision in the flesh of each cutlet, from the side opposite the bone, to make a pocket. Stuff the pocket with the ham, sage and cheese, then press together to seal the sides. Dip the cutlets in the egg first, then coat well with breadcrumbs.

Pour enough olive oil into a large frying pan to cover the base generously and heat gently. Fry the cutlets until golden brown on each side; about 5–6 minutes each side if you like them juicy as I do. Drain on paper towel.

Serve with zucchini and green beans with mint.

ZUCCHINI AND GREEN BEANS WITH MINT

200g green beans, trimmed

300g small zucchini, trimmed and quartered lengthways

3 cloves garlic, halved and roughly sliced

1 bunch fresh mint leaves

½ cup (125ml) extra virgin olive oil

1 tablespoon white wine vinegar or juice of ½ lemon

zucchini and green beans with mint

Beans with mint and garlic are a favourite of mine to accompany a steak or a lamb cutlet, and the combination here of beans with zucchini is even better. The Italians tend to cook their vegetables more than other people – and certainly don't serve them almost raw as the French would. They need to be at the most *al dente*, or 'to the tooth'. What you do is stick the tip of a sharp knife into the vegetable: if it is still a bit crunchy, cook a little longer; if there is little resistance, it should be ready. But ultimately it is all a matter of taste …

serves 4

In a large saucepan, cook the beans and zucchini in lightly salted boiling water until *al dente,* about 15 minutes. Drain, and while still warm put in a bowl. Add the garlic, mint and oil, season with salt and pepper to taste, and then mix in the vinegar or lemon juice.

Leave at room temperature, uncovered, for about half an hour to let the vegetables absorb the flavours. The longer you leave them to infuse, the darker, softer and more garlicky they will become. If eating them by themselves, or with other *antipasti,* eat with some good bread.

If there are any leftovers – unlikely! – then you can happily eat them the next day, so long as they have been chilled overnight.

— *Antonio Carluccio*

Antonio Carluccio

Antonio Carluccio is everything you would expect him to be – a large teddy bear with a head full of cherubic curls, oozing buckets of charm. If meeting the man wasn't enough, being able to cook with this gastronomic giant, the godfather of Italian cuisine, was truly a memorable experience. The first time I watched Antonio Carluccio on TV was about 8 years ago, and right away his food philosophy resonated with me. He's not one for any amount of fuss and stays true to his cooking motto, always – MOF: 'minimum of fuss, maximum of flavour'. It is no wonder he was awarded the Commendatore OMRI in 1998 by the President of Italy for services to Italian gastronomy. My dream is to one day go mushroom hunting with Antonio.

FUN FACTS:

- Antonio began cooking when he was a student of languages in Vienna — to impress the ladies of course.

- His TV career began from coming runner-up in a cooking competition, like someone else I know!

- Antonio loves telling naughty jokes!

When we cooked together
I made mock meat with
mushrooms and Antonio
cooked stuffed lamb cutlets
and pears in red wine.

spice

Indian ❧ Thai ❧ Malaysian

lamb, chickpea and plum korma

This is a rich braised curry of contrasting ingredients.

40g ghee

4 whole green cardamom pods

4 whole cloves

3 whole black cardamom pods

2 bay leaves

1 cinnamon stick

1 onion, thinly sliced

3cm piece (20g) ginger, finely
chopped

3 cloves garlic, minced to a paste

1 tablespoon cumin seeds, roasted
and ground

1 tablespoon coriander seeds,
roasted and ground

1 teaspoon kashmiri red chilli
powder

½ cup plain yoghurt

1kg diced forequarter of lamb or
4 diced lamb shanks

6 plums, stones removed

1 cup (250ml) water

½ cup cooked chickpeas

serves 4

In a large saucepan, heat the ghee over medium heat. Add the spices and onion and cook for 3–4 minutes or until golden brown. Add the ginger and garlic and cook for a further minute. Mix the ground cumin, coriander and chilli powder with the yoghurt and add to the onion mixture. Cook for 3 minutes, or until the oil separates from the spice blend. Increase the heat to high, add the meat and brown.

Stir in the plums and water. Cook, covered, for 1 hour, or until the meat is almost tender. Add the chickpeas, and if needed a little more water, continue to cook for a further 30 minutes, or until the meat is very tender. Rest for 30 minutes before serving.

GREEN LENTIL PARATHA

½ cup (100g) green lentils

2 cups (400g) atta flour, plus extra
for dusting

1 teaspoon salt

½ cup (125ml) melted ghee

¾–1 cup (180–250ml) warm water

green lentil paratha

Homestyle Indian flaky bread with lentils.

serves 4

Soak the lentils in cold water for 6 hours. Drain well.

Combine the flour, lentils, salt, 2 tablespoons melted ghee and enough warm water to make a pliable dough. Mix the dough with a large wooden spoon and knead for a few minutes until the dough comes together. Rest for half an hour.

Divide the dough into little balls, roll out gently, dusting with atta flour to obtain a round shape. Heat a heavy-based frying pan over medium heat and dry pan fry for 2–3 minutes on each side until golden. Brush the paratha with the remaining ghee and cook either side for a few seconds before serving.

1 whole head broccoli (about 350g)

50g panir cheese

1 tablespoon nuts

1 tablespoon chopped raisins

1 teaspoon deseeded chopped green chilli

3 tablespoons coriander leaves, chopped

100g mature Cheddar cheese, grated

1 large free-range egg

1 teaspoon finely chopped ginger

100g hung yoghurt

100ml pouring cream

1 teaspoon ground green cardamom

½ teaspoon ground mace

lemon juice, to serve

tandoori broccoli

Broccoli filled with a panir cheese, dried fruit and nuts then roasted.

serves 4

Cut the broccoli lengthways into four. Place in a heatproof bowl, cover with boiling water and set aside for 3–4 minutes. Drain.

Mix the panir cheese, nuts, raisins, chopped chilli and coriander to make a filling. Place this between the broccoli florets.

Make the marinade by first mixing together the grated cheese and egg, then add the ginger, yoghurt, cream, cardarmom, mace and some salt. Pour the marinade over the broccoli. Place in the fridge for 30 minutes.

Heat the oven to 200°C (190°C fan forced) or the grill to high.

Grill or roast the broccoli until lightly browned, about 7–10 minutes.

Serve hot with a squeeze of lemon juice.

— Ragini Dey

An Indian spice mill in Penang where they still grind spices and flour to order for domestic use.

Ragini Dey

Ragini Dey is spirited, generous and very cheeky. She's so quick-witted that I often almost miss her wicked, under-the-breath remarks. What I love is that she was trailblazing the moment she arrived in Australia, teaching Indian cooking classes when most housewives were dishing up retro nightmares, and then years later introducing Sunday curry instead of traditional roast to South Australia's Government House during the Dunstan era. I do love a bit of a rebel! Her impressive academic background is absolutely reflected in her astounding knowledge of all things spice, and it's not just contained within Indian cuisine. What I've learnt from Ragini is that you can be respectful of history and tradition but still be progressive. It's largely what being a cook in Australia means to me.

FUN FACTS:

- Ragini's husband is also an Indian chef.

- Her most adventurous dish to date is a beef and beetroot vindaloo.

- Before turning her hand to chefing, Ragini was an honours graduate of political science.

This day was all about kormas and debunking the myth that Indian is complicated. Oh, and also that 'tandoori' is about the oven, not red chicken!

chicken and pistachio korma

4 onions, quartered

1¼ cups (312ml) water

¾ cup freshly deshelled salted pistachio

4 large green chillies (taste first and adjust accordingly)

1½ tablespoons vegetable oil or good quality ghee

1½ tablespoons equal parts ginger and garlic paste using a mortar and pestle or very finely chopped

1 tablespoon ground coriander

1 teaspoon ground white pepper

1kg chicken thigh fillets, skin and fat removed, diced

¼ cup (60ml) yoghurt

½ cup (125ml) pouring cream

1 teaspoon garam masala

This recipe was given to me by Ragini Dey, as proof that Indian doesn't have to be complicated to cook, nor is it always laden with assaulting spices. This dish is foolproof, beautifully aromatic and a definite crowd pleaser.

serves 4

Place the onions and 1 cup (250ml) of the water in a saucepan, cover and cook until tender. Drain, cool and puree with a stick blender.

Keep a few pistachios aside for garnishing and place the rest in a food processor and blitz with the green chillies to a coarse paste. Set aside.

Heat the oil or ghee in a frying pan over medium heat, add the onion puree and cook for 4 minutes, do not brown. Add the ginger and garlic paste and sauté for 1 minute. Stir in the coriander and pepper, add the pistachio and green chilli paste and cook for about a minute, or until fragrant.

Add the chicken with remaining water and simmer for 15–20 minutes, or until the chicken is tender. Stir in the yoghurt and cook for a further 2 minutes.

Add the cream and garam masala. Garnish with the reserved pistachios and serve hot with tomato rice.

— *Ragini Dey*

TOMATO RICE

1 tablespoon ghee or butter

1 clove garlic, finely chopped

1 brown onion, chopped

2 cups long grain or basmati rice washed and drained

1 tablespoon tomato paste

1 teaspoon salt

2 pandan leaves, torn into thin strips and tied into a loose knot

water

tomato rice

In a medium to large frying pan, melt the ghee or the butter over medium heat Add the garlic and the onion and sauté until soft and caramelised. Add the rice and coat with the ghee or butter. Stir in the tomato paste and salt.

Transfer the rice mixture to a medium non-stick saucepan and smooth the rice so it is level all over. Cover with water to a depth of 2.5cm above the surface of the rice. Nestle the pandan leaf into the rice and then jiggle the pot around to level the rice again. Bring to the boil, cover and immediately lower to a simmer for 10 minutes. Turn the heat off but leave the saucepan on the stove for a further 15 minutes. It will keep warm covered for up to 2 hours. Fluff up with a spatula or fork before serving.

green beef curry

Green curry paste

1 teaspoon coriander seeds

generous $\frac{1}{2}$ teaspoon cumin seeds

2 Thai cardamom pods

10 white peppercorns

good pinch of grated nutmeg

20–30 small green bird's-eye chillies
   (about 1 tablespoon)

1 long green chilli, deseeded and
   roughly chopped (optional)

good pinch of salt

2 tablespoons chopped lemongrass

1 tablespoon chopped galangal

3 tablespoons chopped garlic

1 teaspoon finely grated kaffir lime
   zest

2 teaspoons chopped red turmeric

1 teaspoon cleaned and chopped
   coriander roots

$\frac{1}{2}$ teaspoon Thai shrimp paste
   (gapi)

For this recipe first make the green curry paste, then braise the beef and finally put it altogether to make a delicious beef curry.

serves 4–6

GREEN CURRY PASTE

In a heavy-based frying pan, separately dry-roast the coriander seeds, cumin seeds and cardamom pods, shaking the pan to prevent the spices from scorching, until aromatic. Husk the cardamom, then grind to a powder with the coriander and cumin seeds, peppercorns and nutmeg, using an electric spice grinder or a pestle and mortar. Set aside.

Using a pestle and mortar, pound the chillies with the salt, then add the remaining ingredients in the order they are listed, reducing each one to a fine paste before adding the next. Alternatively, puree the ingredients in a blender. It will probably be necessary to add a little water to aid the blending, but try not to add more than necessary, as this will dilute the paste and alter the taste of the curry. Halfway through, turn the machine off and scrape down the sides of the bowl with a spatula, whiz until completely pureed. Finally, stir in the ground spices.

Braised beef

1 cup (250ml) coconut cream

good pinch of salt

250g beef (flank, brisket or rump), cut into 5mm thick slices about 2cm x 1cm

1 stalk lemongrass, bruised

2 red eschalots, bruised (optional)

2 Thai cardamom pods, roasted (optional)

1 Thai cardamom leaf or dried bay leaf, roasted (optional)

about 2½ cups (750ml) coconut milk or water

1 tablespoon fish sauce

Curry

1 cup (250ml) coconut cream

1-2 tablespoons fish sauce, more if wanted

1 cup (250ml) coconut milk or water

3-4 kaffir lime leaves, torn into large pieces

pinch of roasted chilli powder, to taste

10-15 small green bird's eye chillies, to garnish

steamed jasmine rice, kanom jin noodles or roti, to serve

BRAISED BEEF

Simmer the coconut cream with the salt and, when thickened slightly and beginning to separate, add the beef and lemongrass, along with the eschalots and spices, if using. Moisten with some of the coconut milk or water and add the fish sauce. Continue to simmer gently, stirring regularly, until the coconut is absorbed and the beef is tender yet still a little resilient: this should take about 20 minutes or so, but it will be necessary to moisten with some more coconut milk or water during this time to prevent the meat becoming too dry. Be careful not to braise the beef until it is falling apart, or it will have a stringy texture. Once the beef is cooked, drain off the excess oil, keeping if for the next stage, and pick out the lemongrass and spices. Cover and set aside. Try to resist eating more than a few delectable slices of the beef – in fact, put it out of reach!

CURRY

Heat a few tablespoons of the reserved oil with the coconut cream and fry the green curry paste over medium heat for 8-10 minutes, stirring often to prevent it from catching. When it is rich and aromatic and quite oily, add the fish sauce and simmer for a minute before adding the coconut milk or water. Simmer for 2-3 minutes before adding the braised beef and the kaffir lime leaves, then continue to simmer for another 10 minutes or longer – until the curry is quite thick, rich and creamy. It may be necessary to add some more coconut milk or water. Check the seasoning – the curry should taste rich, hot, spicy and salty. Allow to sit for 20 minutes or so.

On the streets this curry would be eaten at room temperature – and it does taste better this way. If you prefer to reheat it, do so gently, adding the extra coconut cream, along with the roasted chilli powder and green chillies to taste. Serve with steamed jasmine rice, kanom jin noodles or roti (see page 136).

a good pinch of salt

2 scraped coriander roots

4 cloves garlic

4–5 grilled red eschalots, peeled

around 9 bird's eye chillies,
    depending on the mood

½ teaspoon Thai shrimp paste
    (gapi)

a few tablespoons of chicken stock
    (see page 49)

1–2 tablespoons grated palm sugar

a little tamarind water

½ tablespoon lime juice

a little fish sauce

2 tablespoons pea eggplants

1½ cups small green prawns, peeled,
    deveined and blanched

spicy relish of prawns, shrimp paste and pea eggplants

Using a pestle and mortar, pound the salt, coriander roots and garlic to make a paste. Add the eschalots, chillies and shrimp paste. Pound again until almost pureed. Moisten with the stock. Season with the sugar, tamarind water and lime juice. Carefully add a little fish sauce to taste – do not add too much as there is already a lot of salt present. Add the pea eggplants and bruise slightly before mixing in the prawns.

This spicy relish (*nahm prik*) should be quite thick, hot and salty, sour and sweet.

Serve with some of the following: raw cucumbers and green tomatoes; blanched wing or green beans; blanched dork kae; blanched bamboo with coconut cream.

— *David Thompson*

David Thompson

David Thompson does not suffer fools, and on our first meeting I have to admit to being a little scared … I've heard things about his uncompromising ways, but I've always admired that in a person. He maintains a super-dry wit, accompanied by a 'deathly poker face', but I soon saw past it when he began coaching me through his cooking and that incredible wealth of knowledge came pouring out. His writing on Thai food is so riveting; it made me forever overcome the fear of cooking from a book with not many pictures. He learnt to cook the traditional Thai way from women, not chefs, by watching, touching and tasting. He's very cunning and a bit cruel, and seems to make a habit of feeding people scuds, telling them it won't be that bad. Then just one chuckle will escape from that wicked smile.

FUN FACTS:

• David admits he's no good at throwing roti.

• He laughed when a bit of sliced chilli flew into my eye — mean.

• He hates fusion food with vitriolic passion.

That day David Thompson taught me how to cook green beef curry from scratch while I made stir-fried kangkung and roti.

Malaysian chicken or beef satay

20–25 skewers soaked in water
    for 1 hour

1kg chicken thigh fillets or beef
    chuck steak cut into thin slivers
    no longer than 3cm in length

Marinade

2 tablespoons coriander seeds

1 tablespoon cumin seeds

5 red eschalots or 1 red onion,
    chopped

2 cloves garlic, sliced

1 teaspoon ground turmeric or 2cm
    piece fresh turmeric, chopped

4 stalks finely sliced lemongrass,
    white part only and outer leaves
    discarded

1cm piece galangal, skin sliced off,
    chopped as finely as possible

The origin of satay is unclear as versions of it appear in so many cultures. One theory told to me by a Nonya chef, Florence Tan, suggests that it came from Chinese traders who would preserve skewers of meat in brine and then grill them when they arrived on the shores of Malaysia. Interestingly the term 'satay' means 'three pieces' in the Hokkien dialect. This dish is not a complex one to make but like a lot of Malaysian dishes, it's all about getting the ratios right for the beautiful aromatics, exotic rhizomes and spices. In the streets of Malaysia, satays are cooked over smouldering embers which are continuously fanned to infuse the meat with a gorgeous smokiness, but at home, barbecuing or grilling in the oven will work a treat. Of course, the peanut sauce is half the magic, but please don't be deterred by the amount of oil required to cook the sauce, for without it, the sauce will not develop and caramelise properly. If you are concerned, you may scoop some of the oil out after the sauce is cooked. In Australia, satay is most often served as an entrée, but in Malaysia, it's eaten as a meal in itself accompanied by pressed rice, freshly cut cucumber, red onion and pineapple, which add a lovely refreshing zing to the rich, meaty morsels and peanut sauce. Begin this recipe the day before.

makes 20 skewers, serves 4

To prepare the marinade, dry-roast the coriander and cumin seeds in a small frying pan over medium-high heat, until fragrant and just beginning to smoke. Grind in an electric spice grinder or pound using a mortar and pestle. Set aside.

In a mini food processor, blitz the eschalots or onion, garlic, turmeric (only if fresh), lemongrass and galangal, adding small amounts at a time to achieve a fine paste, or pound thoroughly with a mortar and pestle to a fine paste (see note below). Add the ground coriander and cumin to the wet spice paste and stir to incorporate.

Tip all the meat and the marinade into a snaplock plastic bag. Jiggle the meat around to ensure every piece is coated with the marinade. Push all the air out of the bag and seal. Refrigerate for at least 5 hours, or overnight.

NOTE: Watch that any spice paste containing lemongrass, galangal and dried chillies is adequately broken down as they don't soften much from cooking and create an unpleasant splintery mouthfeel.

Homemade satay sauce

(makes 1 litre, see note below)

15 red eschalots or 2 medium red onions, chopped

8 cloves garlic, chopped

2cm piece galangal, chopped

20 dried long red chillies, stalks discarded, deseeded, soaked in boiling water until soft and drained

2 stalks lemongrass, finely chopped, pale part only, outer layers discarded

1 tablespoon heaped tamarind pulp soaked in $1/3$ cup warm water, or 1–$1\frac{1}{2}$ tablespoons tamarind paste from a jar

200ml vegetable or peanut oil

4 cups (1 litre) water

$1\frac{1}{2}$ tablespoons lime juice, or to taste

$2/3$ cup (130g) brown sugar

1 teaspoon salt

500g salted, roasted, crushed peanuts

....

NOTE: This sauce makes twice the amount you will need but it doesn't really work to make less. It is however, freezer friendly.

....

Thread 3–5 pieces of the meat lengthways onto each skewer, making sure each piece sits flat. This makes it very easy to barbecue or grill as you'll only need to briefly cook the skewers on 2 flat sides, which will ensure the meat is tender and moist.

HOMEMADE SATAY SAUCE

Using a mini food processor, blitz the eschalots, garlic, galangal, rehydrated chillies and lemongrass in small batches to achieve a fine paste. Please be patient and don't be tempted to add water as this will make the paste difficult to caramelise. You can instead use a mortar and pestle but you must add only small amounts of the ingredients at a time, ensuring you have a fine paste before you add more ingredients. Set aside.

To extract the tamarind paste from the pulp, place the pulp in the warm water and mash and stir the mixture with a fork or squeeze with your hands, so the water and pulp become homogenised. Using a rubber spatula, push the pulp through a sieve and into a small bowl. This will catch all the pulp and seeds. Make sure you scrape the bottom of the sieve as the paste is a little sticky and most of it won' t fall into the bowl underneath without your help. Discard the pulp and seeds and reserve the paste until required. You only need 1–2 tablespoons for this recipe, so any unused paste may be frozen in tablespoon portions in an ice cube tray.

Heat oil in a heavy-based non-stick saucepan or wok over medium heat and pour the spice paste in. Stir continuously to make sure it doesn't catch, and cook until there is very little steam rising from the sauce. At this stage the oil will have split from the spice paste and be pooling around the edges of the pan. The sauce will also be getting darker, caramelising, and it will be getting very fragrant.

Add the water and bring to the boil. Add the tamarind, lime juice, sugar salt and half the peanuts. Bring to the boil again, remove from the heat and set aside until required. You can make this a couple of days ahead and keep it in a glass jar in the fridge and then reheat before serving. Add the remaining nuts and stir just before you serve as this will give it a nice bit of crunch. Season further with salt and more lime juice if required.

KETUPAT (COMPRESSED RICE CAKES)

2 cups (400g) jasmine rice, washed and drained

1.4 litres water

1 pandan leaf, torn into thin strips and loosely knotted (optional)

FRUIT SKEWERS

½ fresh pineapple, core removed, cut into bite size pieces

1 red onion, cut into 2cm cubes with layers separated

1 continental cucumber, halved lengthways, sliced into 1cm pieces

ketupat (compressed rice cakes)

Place the rice in a medium, non-stick saucepan. Make sure the surface of the rice is as flat as possible. Cover the rice with water so it comes 5cm above the surface of the rice. Add the pandan leaf and bring to the boil. Cover, lower heat and simmer for 10 minutes. Turn off the heat but leave the saucepan to sit on the hotplate for another 15 minutes.

Turn out the rice into a 33 x 23cm (or similar size) baking dish lined with foil. The rice will still be hot, so loosely cover it with clingfilm and then use a tea towel to protect your palms from the heat while you firmly press the rice down to evenly spread to a 2cm thickness. Cool completely for 3–4 hours to room temperature (do not refrigerate, as this will make the rice go hard), then invert the dish and place the rice on a chopping board. Discard the foil. With a sharp, wet knife cut the rice into 2cm cubes and serve in a bowl to go with the satay.

fruit skewers

Skewer the pineapple, onion and cucumber, alternating all the way along.

These are eaten with the satay and ketupat, all of which are dipped into the satay sauce. If you can't be bothered skewering them, just plonk them in separate bowls for your guests to serve themselves.

serunding daging
beef floss rendang with turmeric rice

500g blade or skirt steak with sinews trimmed, cut along the grain into 4 pieces

1 cup (90g) desiccated coconut

2 tablespoons coriander seeds

1 tablespoon cumin seeds

1 tablespoon fennel seeds

2 cups (500ml) coconut milk

2 tablespoons sugar

1 teaspoon salt

Rempah (spice paste)

5-6 long dried red chillies, deseeded and soaked in hot water, drained

1cm piece (10g) galangal, skin sliced off, chopped as finely as possible

10 (100g) red eschalots, roughly chopped

3 cloves garlic, sliced

3cm piece (20g) ginger, sliced

3 stalks lemongrass, pale part only, outer leaves discarded, finely sliced

3 limes, cut into wedges

coriander sprigs, to garnish

Serunding daging is the Malay name for what is best described as a dry, beef floss curry. I didn't grow up eating this dish but discovered it while researching Nonya food and found it a fascinating alternative to a saucy curry. The process and ingredients are in fact very similar to one of Malaysia's favourite dishes, beef rendang, but instead of cutting raw meat into chunks and braising it in the curry sauce, you pre-boil it until it is very tender and then shred or floss the beef very finely. This is then introduced to the spices, aromatics and lots of coconut flesh and milk, and reduced to caramelise to the point of almost being crispy. You will find it is a very rich dish, full of exotic nuances, which makes the dish more appropriate as a sharing dish or as an entrée.

serves 5-6 for entree or as part of a shared meal

In a small saucepan cover the beef with water and simmer for about 1 hour, or until the beef is very tender. Drain and immediately shred as finely as possible with 2 forks.

Meanwhile, in a large non-stick frying pan, dry toast the desiccated coconut on medium heat until it turns auburn brown. Place in a food processor and blitz to a grainy paste. In Malaysian cookery this paste is called kirisik. Set aside.

Quickly clean the frying pan with a paper towel and re-use. On medium-high heat, dry toast the coriander, cumin and fennel seeds, until very fragrant and just beginning to smoke. Immediately put into a mortar and pestle to pound to a powder, or grind to a powder in an electric spice grinder. Set aside.

To make the rempah or spice paste, blitz all the aromatics – chilli, galangal, eschalots, garlic, ginger and lemongrass – in a mini food processor to a fine paste. Do not add water, instead blend by adding small amounts at a time. The woodier aromatics must be very finely chopped for this. You can use a mortar and pestle, but only add a small handful of aromatics each time, making sure the ingredients have been pounded to a fine paste before you add any more.

Combine all the ingredients in a frying pan and keep stirring and toasting the beef until it becomes very dry, dark brown and crispy.

Serve about ¼ cup of the meat on a scant ½ cup of turmeric rice accompanied by a wedge of lime. Garnish with coriander.

280g glutinous rice, washed and drained

1 slice tamarind (sometimes called assam), not the pulp

1 cup (250ml) coconut milk

½ teaspoon salt

1 teaspoon ground turmeric

2 pandan leaves, torn into thin slivers and loosely knotted

turmeric rice

This turmeric glutinous rice is the most favoured accompaniment for dry beef floss curry as its stickiness contrasts nicely with the texture of the beef. It's not traditional but I like to serve the dish with wedges of lime to add moisture, and acid to cut through the richness of the coconut and plentiful spices.

Begin this recipe the day before.

Soak the rice overnight in water with the slice of tamarind. The tamarind cuts through the richness of the rice and gives it a nice gloss when served.

Remove the tamarind. Drain the rice for 5 minutes in a sieve, and then pour into a round cake tin. Mix the coconut milk, salt, turmeric and pandan leaves into the rice and steam for 15–20 minutes on high heat, or until the rice is tender. For this you need a wok or large saucepan and a metal trivet or anything that'll let steam pass through (available at Asian grocers) which the cake tin stands on. Fill the wok or pan so there's a 2.5cm space between the bottom of the tin and the water. If using a wok, it must have a domed lid so the steam can circulate over the tin. If using a pan, it must have high enough sides to use a flat lid.

Turn the heat off, loosen the grains with a fork or chopsticks and cover with foil until required.

During my trip to a kampung (village) in Melaka, Malaysia. Here turmeric glutinous rice is cooked in bamboo lined with banana leaves and smoked; it's usually reserved for special occasions. When cooked the cylinders of rice are cut into discs to serve.

nonya chicken curry with roti chanai

3 tablespoons coriander seeds

1 teaspoon cumin seeds

1 teaspoon fennel seeds

4 tablespoons vegetable oil

1 star anise

2 whole cloves

1 cinnamon stick

100ml coconut cream

6–7 sprigs of curry leaves

1.5kg chicken thigh fillets

300g baby chat potatoes, peeled and halved

2 bird's-eye chillies, deseeded and halved lengthways

400ml coconut milk

2 teaspoons salt, or to taste

1 teaspoon sugar

Rempah (spice paste)

15 long dried red chillies, deseeded, soaked in hot water, drained and chopped

270g red eschalots, roughly chopped

3 cloves garlic, sliced

20g belachan, toasted (see note page 44)

25g fresh turmeric root, chopped

You don't get more definitively Malaysian than this classic Nonya dish. It is the mainstay of every Malaysian pot-luck dinner and the most out of place dish at our Christmas buffet table but there it always is right next to the ham. Hilarious! The first time I made this and it worked, and I jumped around like a lunatic, I was so happy. I felt like I had conjured magic. To make a dish like this and have it hitting all those familiar notes of home, was a complete thrill.

serves 5–6

Dry toast the coriander, cumin and fennel seeds in a small frying pan until fragrant and beginning to smoke. Tip into a mortar and pestle or an electric spice grinder and grind to a powder. Set aside.

If you are using the traditional mortar and pestle method to make the rempah or spice paste, start by pounding a small amount of the prepared dried chillies, adding small handfuls at a time and pounding thoroughly into a fine paste. Next add in small quantities the eschalots, garlic, belachan and turmeric and pound in the same manner until it becomes a homogenous fine paste. If using a mini food processor, still exercise the same patience and pulverise by adding small amounts of the ingredients at a time to achieve a fine paste without adding water.

Heat the vegetable oil in a heavy-based non-stick saucepan or wok, on a medium heat. Toast the star anise, cloves and cinnamon stick for about 20 seconds. Add the rempah or spice paste and sauté for about 6–10 minutes, or until the sauce becomes very fragrant and emitting very little steam. Add the toasted dry spices, coconut cream and curry leaves, and keep cooking until very fragrant. You will know when the mixture is ready when the oil begins to separate from the mixture.

Add the chicken pieces and stir for 1 minute. Add the potatoes, chillies, coconut milk, salt and sugar. Cover and simmer until the chicken and potatoes are tender. Serve with roti and/or steamed jasmine rice.

4 cups (500g) plain flour

1 teaspoon salt

1 teaspoon sugar

1¼ cups (310ml) water, add extra if dough seems dry

1½ tablespoons condensed milk

1½ tablespoons margarine, at room temperature

½ large free-range egg, lightly whisked

extra margarine

extra vegetable oil

roti chanai

The perfect roti recipe had been eluding me until I met Kuala Lumpur's Chef Matt of Roti Chanai fame. He's been making Malaysian roti since age 9, so it's no mystery why he's such an expert. The only problem with characters like him is that all his cooking is done by sight and feel and the quantities estimated, so I had to scribble down the recipe as best as I could on the fly.

makes 10–12

Begin the recipe the day before.

Combine the flour, salt and sugar in a large mixing bowl. Make a well in the centre of the dry ingredients and into it pour the water, condensed milk, margarine and egg. Work in a circular motion with your hands, gradually gathering more and more of the flour into the wet ingredients until you more or less have a single mass. Tip all the ingredients onto the bench and knead until smooth and elastic. Roll into a cylinder and divide the dough into 10 pieces. Knead each piece a few times to achieve a smooth texture, then shape into a ball. Gently and generously coat each ball with margarine and place the balls in a bowl sitting next to each other. Cover with clingfilm and allow to rest at room temperature, overnight.

After resting, the dough should be soft and stretchy. Now the fun part begins. Start by oiling a substantial area of the bench liberally. Place one of the balls of dough onto the table and press down with the palm of your hand while moving it in a circular motion. This is just to flatten and smooth out the surface of the dough as much as possible before you stretch it. It takes a bit of practice to throw the roti the professional way and while it's definitely quicker, an equally effective method is to work around the edges of the circle of dough, gently stretching the edges outwards as far and as thinly as you can (so it is like tracing paper and about 60–70cm in diameter), before holes start to appear.

Overlap the sides into the middle so you have 3 layers of roti on top of each other, then fold this elongated shape into thirds again, so you end up with a 6-layered squarish shaped roti. Heat up your frypan on high heat with a dash of vegetable oil and panfry the roti until golden blisters appear on both sides. When cooked, immediately slide the roti onto a chopping board, wrap your palms around the edges and smash your hands together so the roti bunches up and flakes. Rotate the roti and do this several times while it is still hot. Serve immediately with curry.

TIP: Before each fold, gently smear a small dollop (about ¼ of teaspoon) of margarine onto the roti. This will prevent the layers from sticking and help the roti to cook more evenly.

A roadside coffee shop in a Melaka kampung serving roti.

steamed 5-spice taro cake

This is a classic Hakka dish that I saw a lot of as a child. It's one of my mum's favourites, and no one makes it like her. It's also a great demonstration of classic Chinese technique with a combination of stir-frying first and then steaming.

1½ cups (265g) rice flour

½ cup (60g) cornflour

4 cups (1 litre) water

3 tablespoons vegetable or peanut oil

2 lap cheong (Chinese sausage), finely chopped

1 cup (80g) firmly packed dried shrimp, soaked in boiling water for 10 minutes, squeezed and finely chopped or pulsed in a food processor

400g taro, diced into 1cm cubes

1 teaspoon 5-spice powder

1 teaspoon salt

1 teaspoon sugar

⅓ cup chopped spring onions

2–3 tablespoons roasted peanuts, crushed

2–3 tablespoons deep-fried red eschalots (from Asian grocers)

1 mild red chilli, deseeded and finely chopped

Garlic chilli sauce (makes 1 cup)

10 long, red chillies, deseeded and roughly chopped

½ head of garlic cloves, peeled

2 tablespoons white vinegar

½ teaspoon salt

1–2 teaspoons sugar

2 tablespoons tomato ketchup

3 tablespoons peanut oil

serves 8–10 as an entrée or snack

Make sure you have a wok and domed lid big enough to fit a 22–23cm round springform cake tin. Place a cooling rack or metal trivet in the wok to sit the baking tin on. Fill with enough water so it comes to 2cm below the rack. Bring the water to a gentle simmer.

With a wooden spoon or whisk, mix the rice flour and cornflour with the water to make a thin batter.

In a wok or large frying pan, sauté the lap cheong in the oil to render some of the fat out of the sausage. Then add the shrimp and cook until slightly coloured and fragrant, about 2 minutes. At this point, the oil should start to foam a little. Add the taro, 5-spice powder, salt, sugar and the batter. Cook on medium heat, stirring and scraping the sides of the pan continuously for about 3 minutes, or until the mixture is a thick starchy paste. Taste and further season if necessary.

Transfer the mixture to a greased springform cake tin, using a spatula to smooth the surface.

Bring the water in the wok to a boil. Place the cake tin on the trivet and steam the cake with the lid on the wok for about 40–45 minutes. Don't worry if the cake looks a little wobbly when it comes out of the wok, it will firm up as it cools.

Immediately sprinkle the spring onions, peanuts, eschalots and chilli over the top and allow the cake to cool to room temperature. Traditionally, my mum would cut these into bite sized diamonds and then arrange these pieces into a snowflake-like design. Serve warm or at room temperature with homemade or store-bought Asian style garlic chilli sauce.

To make the chilli sauce, pulverise all the ingredients in a mini food processor to a puree. If you want to store the sauce, tip the mixture into a small pot and bring it to the boil. Cool and store in a glass jar in the fridge for up to 2 weeks.

My trip to Kuala Lumpur

My first day in KL was all about family and food. All the womenfolk got together to cook up a storm at my grandma's house — a perfect way to have a reunion. I'd forgotten how unrelenting the tropical heat was and was positively wilting especially when I got near the stove.

DAY 1

Me at Grandma's house with Mum (right) and Great Auntie Sook Poh who's a brilliant cook and today she coaches me through making popiah.

Popiah is a dish I usually associate with the paternal side of my family as it is a Hokkien dish. Here I'm slicing cucumber after turning them into ribbons.

The ingredients for popiah are essentially a fresh spring roll, filled with a yam bean stir-fry.

My grandma, great auntie and I having a refreshment of chendol, a cool sweet soup of coconut, palm sugar and pandan-flavoured noodles.

The reunion was all girlpower. Some of these 'little aunties' I hadn't seen for over a decade.

My mum had just told me off for being a glutton.

Showing my granny some pictures I'd taken of KL. In the background, another great aunt.

On my way to see Chef Ismael and poke my nose through his huge restaurant which specialises in traditional Malay dishes.

Everyday the restaurant offers up the most unbelievable smorgasbord, so the restaurant has many kitchens and cooks.

I'd seen these river snails at the market and having never tried them before, I begged Chef Ismael to cook them for me.

As a special treat, Chef Ismael had organised a mock Malay wedding the night I was visiting. The wedding was incredibly colourful and joyfully noisy, followed by karaoke of course!

DAY 3

At a specialist durian dessert house – I love the stuff especially the little durians from the kampungs. Sweet and custardy but definitely an acquired taste.

It was a pleasure to meet Chef Shamil whose restaurant specialises in Nasi Lemak, one of Malaysia's favourite dishes.

The night eating was spectacular. This is what I came home for. The only problem is too much choice and only one stomach.

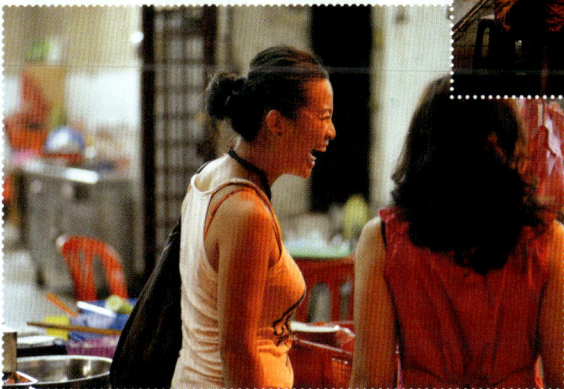

Here I'm having some frog congee. After much perusing and full of indecision, I settled on a dish I'd never tried before — yes it tasted like chicken but perhaps a touch earthier.

rice, noodles and stir-fries

nonya fried rice

1 cup (200g) raw jasmine rice, cooked and refrigerated overnight

⅓ cup (80ml) vegetable oil

¾ cup dried shrimp, soaked in boiling water for 10–15 minutes, drained and pounded in a mortar and pestle or blitzed in a food processor to a crumbly consistency

160g peeled uncooked prawn flesh, cut into small pieces

2 tablespoons light soy sauce

¼ teaspoon white pepper

1 teaspoon salt

1 teaspoon sugar

2 large free-range eggs, lightly beaten

1 telegraph cucumber, quartered lengthways, seeds sliced out, cut diagonally into 2–3 mm slices

Rempah (spice paste)

2 large long red chillies, deseeded, or 8 dried chillies deseeded, soaked in boiling water and drained

3 cloves garlic, sliced

6 large red eschalots, roughly chopped

Begin this recipe the day before.

This is definitely a dish I associate with my koo poh (great aunt), who is one of my great cooking heroes. It's not your usual Chinese-style chop-shop fried rice filled with odds and ends from the fridge, but a Nonya-style one with a very distinct flavour profile of dried shrimp and that classic Malaysian combination of eschalot, garlic and dried chilli aromas. I have many memories of my aunt making it way too hot for me but still scarfing it down in spite of the heat because it is just so delicious. The addition of crunchy, refreshing cucumber at the very end is quite unexpected but definitely inspired!

serves 2

Begin by making the rempah. If you are using a mortar and pestle, begin with pounding the chillies, then add the garlic and eschalots. Continue pounding until a paste forms. If using a food processor, blitz everything together in one fell swoop.

Heat the oil in a wok or large non-stick frying pan on medium heat and add the rempah. Sauté until fragrant and caramelised. You will know the paste is ready when very little steam rises from the wok and the colour deepens. Add the pounded dried shrimp and stir-fry until fragrant and slightly toasted, about 1 minute. Add the prawns and stir-fry until just cooked. Then immediately add the rice, soy sauce, pepper, salt and sugar. Cook until the grains of rice have separated, and heated through.

Make a well in the middle of the wok by pushing the rice to the side. Tip in the egg and let it sit for about 10 seconds so the bottom caramelises. With an eggflip, flip the egg over, chop it up with the eggflip, and mix through the rice. Cook for a further 10-20 seconds.

Add the sliced cucumber and toss, until everything is incorporated. Serve hot or at room temperature.

TIP: The trick to cooking great fried rice is refrigerating the rice overnight first! It keeps the grains separate and the dish from getting stodgy.

chop-shop fried rice

1 cup (200g) raw jasmine rice, cooked and refrigerated overnight

¼ cup (60ml) vegetable or peanut oil

2 medium brown onions, finely chopped

2 lap cheong (Chinese sausage), sliced 3mm thick

1 chicken breast fillet (about 250g), diced into 1cm cubes

½ cup (80g) frozen peas

½ cup (80g) carrot, diced into 5mm cubes

200g peeled uncooked prawn flesh, cut into small pieces

½ teaspoon salt

2 tablespoons light soy sauce

¼ teaspoon white pepper

3 large free-range eggs, lightly beaten

pinch of sugar

Begin this recipe the day before.

serves 2

In a wok, heat the oil over medium heat and cook the onion for 2 minutes, or until tender and brown.

Add the lap cheong and stir-fry for a minute to render off some of the fat. Add the chicken breast and stir-fry for 2 minutes, or until lightly browned and cooked.

Add the prawns, carrot and peas and stir-fry for 1 minute, or until the prawns are just cooked.

Add the cooked rice, salt, soy sauce and white pepper and stir-fry until the grains of rice are separate and tender.

Make a well in the middle of the rice by pushing the rice to the edges of the wok. Pour the eggs into the well but don't stir for about 10 seconds. With an eggflip, flip the egg over. It should be nice and brown. Repeat this process until the egg looks nearly cooked. Chop the egg into small pieces with the eggflip. Stir the egg through the rice, add the sugar and cook for another 30 seconds. Serve immediately as a meal in itself.

Thai fried rice

1 cup (200g) raw jasmine rice, cooked and refrigerated overnight

¼ cup (60ml) vegetable oil

8 large red eschalots or 2 red onions, chopped

4 cloves garlic, peeled

1 long red chilli, finely chopped

1 chicken breast fillet (about 250g), diced into 1cm cubes

200g green medium prawns, chopped

2 tablespoons fish sauce

1 tablespoon light soy sauce

¾ cup coriander with stems, cleaned and chopped

½ cup Thai basil, chopped

¼ teaspoon sugar

salt to taste

coriander leaves, to garnish

Begin this recipe the day before.

serves 2

In a wok or large non-stick frying pan, heat the oil over medium heat and sauté the eschalots and garlic for 1–2 minutes, or until very light golden.

Add the chilli and chicken and cook for a further 2 minutes, or until the chicken is golden. Add the prawns and stir-fry for 30 seconds, or until just cooked.

Add the rice, fish sauce, soy sauce and stir-fry until the rice is separate and tender. Add the coriander, basil and sugar and stir-fry until the herbs are well combined. Taste and add more herbs and seasoning if required. Serve as a one-wok meal, garnished with the coriander.

char kwai teow with cubic noodles

Noodles

1 cup (175g) rice flour

⅓ cup (40g) cornflour

½ teaspoon salt

400ml water

Char kwai teow

2 tablespoons light soy

2 teaspoons dark soy

1 teaspoon sugar

10 medium prawns, peeled, deveined and butterflied

100g fish cake sliced or 1 chicken thigh fillet cut into small pieces

150g pork fat

3–4 cloves garlic finely chopped

2 lap cheong (Chinese sausages), sliced into 3mm pieces

2 teaspoons dried chilli flakes

¼ cup shelled pipis (optional)

cubic noodles or 250g fresh flat-ribbon rice noodles

3 large free-range eggs lightly whisked

2 cups bean sprouts

¾ cup Chinese chives cut into 4cm lengths

Marinade

1 teaspoon light soy

1 teaspoon sugar

2 teaspoons shaoxing rice wine

pinch of white pepper

Char kwai teow is one of those indelible dishes that illustrates what the street food culture in Malaysia is all about. This means it's rarely ever cooked at home as the best versions of it are found in the street. It's easy to forget that when a street vendor specialises in a certain dish, he or she has prepped and cooked it a thousand times over, so you're never going to beat that sort of expertise! Kwai teow is also one of those dishes with an uncompromising ingredient list. Miss or substitute one and the dish will miss its mark.

serves 2

NOODLES

It is difficult to find a dish that is the right size, so I simply make one. Mark out a 15cm square on four layers of foil. Fold up the sides, and neatly fold or scrunch (if you're impatient) the corners, so they are secure.

Place a round 25cm cake cooling rack in a wok and fill with water to 2cm below the rack. Heat the water to a gentle simmer, and cover.

Whisk all the ingredients together in a small saucepan. Cook on medium heat, stirring continuously with a wooden spoon until thickened and slightly translucent. Pour into your foil dish and balance on the rack. Cover and steam on high heat for 8–10 minutes, or until the mixture is set enough that it springs back when lightly pressed. Set aside and cool completely for a few hours or overnight, but do not refrigerate.

When the mixture is cool it should be about 1.5cm thick. Cut as precisely as possible into cubes. Set aside.

CHAR KWAI TEOW

Mix the marinade ingredients together and marinate the prawns and chicken (if using) together for 10 minutes. Make sure all your prep is ready as this dish must be done quickly on a high heat on a gas stove.

Mix the seasoning of light soy, dark soy and sugar in a small bowl and set aside.

Dice 100g of the pork fat into 7mm cubes. Fry in a wok over medium heat until golden (no oil is required as some of the pork fat will render down). Drain the pork fat croutons on a paper towel and set aside. If you do not have 3 tablespoons of liquid fat left in the wok, render the remaining 50g of pork fat until you do and save whatever is left over for the next batch.

Divide the rest of the ingredients in half as each individual serve has to be cooked separately to achieve the smoky flavour and to avoid overcrowding in the wok.

Add the garlic and lap cheong to the wok and stir-fry for 7–10 seconds, or until the garlic begins to turn golden. Add the chilli, prawns, chicken (if using) and stir-fry for about 10 seconds or until cooked. Add the fish cake (if using) and pipis and stir-fry for 5 seconds.

Gently separate the cubic or fresh flat-ribbon rice noodles by hand so they are not in a clump. Add to the wok with the light and dark soy sauces and sugar mixture and stir-fry for 10–20 seconds. Push the noodles to the side of the wok and pour the egg into the middle. Let it sit and brown a little, then scramble by making figures-of-8 with an egg flip. Stir-fry until the eggs are cooked then add the sprouts and chives. Stir-fry for a few seconds before adding the white pepper and some salt or sugar if more seasoning is required. Remove from the heat and serve immediately with the pork fat croutons sprinkled on top.

gnocchi with basic tomato and basil sauce

Tomato and basil sauce

2kg vine ripened tomatoes

⅓ cup (80ml) olive oil

8 cloves garlic, finely chopped

1½ teaspoons salt

½ teaspoon sugar

1 handful basil leaves, torn

freshly ground black pepper

This is THE best pasta sauce, ever, as it's so simple, versatile, and just delicious. You can use it with any store-bought pasta, and with a bit of parmigiano-reggiano grated over the top, it's one of my favourite meals. If you reduce it a little further, you will have the perfect pizza sauce.

Here, I've paired it with gnocchi, which is one of those things people always bang on about being hard to master, but it's not the case at all. The most common problem is that a lot of people don't know what the texture of real gnocchi is like, which is soft pillows of potato with just enough flour to bind it all together, not little chewy nuggets made with too much flour. The key is minimal handling. You want to bind all the ingredients together without too much kneading, as overworking the gluten will equal high bounce factor, which isn't desirable at all. Once you build familiarity and instinct with the tactile qualities of what good gnocchi dough should feel like, you'll also understand what being a good cook is all about – tasting, feeling, observing.

serves 6

TOMATO AND BASIL SAUCE

Remove the stems and tops of the tomatoes, score the skin of each tomato all the way round. Place in a bowl and cover with boiling water. Weigh the tomatoes down with a small saucer and wait for 5–10 minutes. Drain the tomatoes, peel and discard the skins. Chop roughly. Set aside.

In a medium saucepan, heat the olive oil and briefly sauté the garlic until aromatic but not at all coloured. Pour in the chopped tomatoes, salt and sugar. Bring to the boil, then lower the heat and simmer for 7 minutes. Add the basil and simmer for another 10 minutes. The sauce should have reduced and thickened. If it is still too watery, simmer to reduce further and add the pepper.

Gnocchi

1kg Dutch creams or kipfler
   potatoes, skins scrubbed
   and left on

200g plain flour

1 large free-range egg, lightly beaten

1 teaspoon salt

100g parmigiano-reggiano (see
   note below) or parmesan cheese,
   finely grated

water

2 teaspoons salt

GNOCCHI

Place the potatoes in a large pot, cover with plenty of water and bring to the boil. Boil until tender and the tip of a knife is easily inserted. Drain and cool briefly. Hold the potatoes with a tea towel or oven mitt in one hand and peel the skin off with the other.

To mash the potatoes, either run through a mouli or a potato ricer or mash with a fork and push through a sieve. Place the mashed potato, flour, egg, salt and cheese in a large bowl. Mix together, then gently knead until just combined. The texture should feel like very soft playdough but it shouldn't stick to your hands. Dust the bench with a small amount of flour, break off small amounts of dough and gently roll into 1cm diameter long tubes. With a knife, cut off 1.5cm sections, roll them in plain flour and rest them on a tray ready to boil.

In a large pot, boil plenty of water with 2 teaspoons of salt. Shake excess flour off the gnocchi before tossing it into the boiling water. When the gnocchi pieces are cooked, they will float to the top. Gently scoop out with a slotted spoon and lower straight into the tomato sauce. Handle the gnocchi tenderly, so you don't end up with a porridge of potato!

Serve in bowls with grated parmigiano-reggiano and a sprinkle of chopped parsley if desired.

NOTE: Parmigiano–reggiano is parmesan cheese made only in the designated Italian regions of Parma, Reggio Emilia, Modena, Bologna and Mastova and is of a very high quality. Any other cheese made in the same style can only be labelled as parmesan.

prawn noodle salad

Salad

600g peeled and deveined green
    prawns, cooked

1 large Lebanese cucumber, peeled
    and cut into strips with a peeler

1 cup (30g) Thai basil leaves

1 cup (30g) coriander leaves

3 tablespoons chopped spring
    onions, white part only

½ red onion, finely sliced

3 tomatoes, deseeded, cut into strips

2 cups cooked rice vermicelli or
    fresh flat-ribbon rice noodles,
    chopped into bite-sized pieces

Dressing

1 tablespoon kecap manis

1 tablespoon sweet chilli sauce

2–3 garlic cloves, crushed

1 teaspoon grated lime or lemon zest

1 tablespoon lime or lemon juice

2 teaspoons minced or pickled ginger

2–3 teaspoons grated palm sugar

1 tablespoon fish sauce

1 teaspoon very finely chopped kaffir
    lime leaves

½ teaspoon white pepper

Optional garnish

chopped spring onions

roasted peanuts

fried eschalots (from Asian grocers)

serves 4–6

Combine the salad ingredients in a large bowl and toss well.

Mix the dressing ingredients and adjust for flavour. Toss together with the prawns.

Serve the salad sprinkled with spring onions, peanuts and eschalots.

Athough this is a recipe for prawns, it could be converted to fish, seafood or other meats.

— Ian Parmenter

kangkung stir-fry with coconut rice

Coconut rice

2 cups (400g) jasmine rice, washed and drained

1½ cups (375ml) coconut milk

300ml water

1 pandan leaf, shredded or torn by hand into strips and tied into a knot

½ teaspoon salt

Kangkung stir-fry

8 red eschalots, roughly chopped

4 garlic cloves, roughly chopped

2 long red chillies, deseeded and roughly chopped

3 teaspoons belachan (see note page 44)

½ cup dried shrimp, soaked in hot water for 10-15 minutes, squeezed and roughly chopped

3-4 tablespoons vegetable oil

1 teaspoon sugar

350g (approximately 2 bunches) kangkung

¼-⅓ cup (60-80ml) water

This is a dish I often order if I eat out, but so much better cooked at home. The dish is meant to be quite salty but like a lot of Asian food, is meant to be eaten sparingly with rice and other sharing dishes. In this case, I've recommended coconut rice, as the richness of the coconut beautifully buffers the salt and chilli content of the dish. There is belachan in this recipe but please don't omit it as it tastes quite contrary to the way it smells. Without it, the dish will lack the depth required to bind all the flavours together.

serves 2 or 4 as part of a shared meal

To make the coconut rice, place the rice in a medium non-stick saucepan. Stir in the remaining ingredients and level out the rice. Bring to the boil, then cover and turn the heat down to a simmer. Simmer for 10 minutes, turn the heat off and then leave on the stove covered for a further 15 minutes. With a fork or chopsticks, fluff up the rice especially the bits on the bottom. If left covered, the rice will keep warm for up to 2 hours.

KANGKUNG STIR-FRY

To make the rempah or spice paste, pound the eschalots, garlic, chilli and belachan to a fine paste. Transfer the spice paste to a small bowl. Now pound the dried shrimp to a crumbly consistency. Alternatively, blitz the spice paste in a mini food processor and then do the same with the dried shrimp.

Heat the oil in a wok over medium heat. First sauté the dried shrimp for about 5 minutes, or until it becomes very fragrant and golden. Add the rempah and stir-fry until it caramelises and becomes very fragrant. When the rempah is cooked, very little steam will rise from it and the oil will begin to split from the paste and pool around the edges of the wok.

To cook the kangkung, snap the entire stalk with leaves attached into 4cm lengths and discard at least 3-4cm at the ends, as these can be fibrous. Toss in to the wok and at the same time pour in ¼ cup of the water to loosen the spice paste so it coats the vegetable. Stir-fry until the kangkung has just wilted. Immediately remove from the heat, and serve with plain or coconut rice.

stir-fries with a difference

Each recipe serves 2. If you make all of these, you'll have yourself a home-style Chinese banquet!

I really wanted to do a stir-fry section because everyone thinks a stir-fry is a no-brainer but this is not the case. In Chinese cooking, stir-frying is an art form that involves recognising and controlling how the intensity of the flame affects each ingredient. Like the specialised culinary vocabulary used in, say, French pastry making, there is a myriad of terms employed to describe the many, many forms of stir-frying. From the order in which the ingredients enter the wok to the way everything is cut is important, and once you learn to appreciate this, that is when you start making real stir-fries. For example, think about how long a vegetable you are pairing with a meat will take to cook. You will probably start with the aromatics, add the meat, then you want to add the veggies that are cut so they require very brief cooking so the meat does not become overdone and the veggies still hold some crunch. You want to add seasoning in the middle or at the end, so the liquid in the meat and veggies don't immediately leach out causing a braising effect rather than a punchy, quick lick of high heat, which will seal the freshness of each ingredient quickly.

Another word of advice, the condiment isle in your local Asian grocer as it's an absolute treasure trove of unusual flavours you can inject into your stir-fries, and don't be put off by the word 'fermented' often written on Chinese packets, it simply means preserved.

Also, a gas flame is a must-have, of course!

BEAN SPROUTS WITH ANCHOVY AND CHILLI

3 tablespoons vegetable oil

3 cloves garlic, finely chopped

25g salted mackerel or 6–7 large anchovies fillets

1 long red chilli, deseeded and finely chopped

500g bean sprouts

1 teaspoon fish sauce

¼ teaspoon sugar

2 handfuls of garlic chives, cut into 4cm lengths

steamed jasmine rice, to serve

CHICKEN WITH TOBAN JIANG

3 tablespoons vegetable oil

2 cloves garlic, finely chopped

250g chicken thigh fillets, cut into small pieces

1 tablespoon toban jiang (chilli bean paste)

¼ teaspoon sugar

1 teaspoon light soy sauce

1 tablespoon shaoxing rice wine

¼ teaspoon sesame oil

1 large red capsicum, cut into 2 x 2cm pieces

6–7 spring onions, green part only, cut into 4cm lengths

½ teaspoon cornflour

1 tablespoon water

steamed jasmine rice, to serve

bean sprouts with anchovy and chilli

serves 2

Heat the oil in a wok over high heat. Reduce the heat to medium and add the garlic. Sauté very briefly until the garlic begins to turn golden.

Add the salted mackerel or anchovies, and stir-fry until golden. While it cooks use a spatula or eggflip to chop and squash to a fine crumbly consistency.

Add chilli, bean sprouts, fish sauce, sugar and garlic chives and stir for 10-20 seconds.

Serve immediately with steamed jasmine rice.

chicken with toban jiang

serves 2

Heat the oil in a wok over high heat. Sauté the garlic very briefly, until it begins to turn golden.

Add the chicken and stir-fry for 2–3 minutes, or until golden. Add the toban jiang, sugar, light soy, shaoxing, sesame oil and capsicum and stir-fry for 10–20 seconds. Add the spring onions and cook for a further 5 seconds, then push ingredients to the side of the wok, making a well in the centre.

Combine the cornflour and water and mix until smooth with no lumps. Pour into the centre of the wok, stir and bring to the boil. Turn the heat off and give the wok a bit of a toss so the sauce coats the ingredients. Transfer on to a plate and garnish with coriander.

Serve immediately with steamed jasmine rice.

PORK AND GARLIC SHOOTS

2 tablespoons vegetable oil

150g minced pork

3 tablespoons Chinese preserved shredded olive

1 tablespoon shaoxing rice wine

1 teaspoon light soy sauce

1/4 teaspoon sugar

1 bunch garlic shoots, cut into 4cm lengths

steamed jasmine rice, to serve

BRUSSELS SPROUTS WITH GINGER AND PRAWNS

220g prawns, peeled, deveined and butterflied

1 teaspoon shaoxing rice wine

pinch of white pepper

1/2 teaspoon sugar

2 1/2 tablespoons vegetable oil

2 cloves garlic, finely chopped

3.5cm piece (25g) ginger, cut into matchsticks

10 Brussels sprouts, halved, shredded

1 teaspoon fish sauce

1 tablespoon oyster sauce

1/4 teaspoon sesame oil

5 spring onions, cut into 4cm lengths

1/2 teaspoon cornflour

1 tablespoon water

handful of coriander sprigs

steamed jasmine rice, to serve

pork and garlic shoots

serves 2

Heat the oil in a wok over high heat. Sauté the minced pork until it develops a little colour, 1–2 minutes.

Chop up the pork mince with a spatula into smaller pieces. Add the preserved olive and stir-fry for 5 seconds.

Add the remaining ingredients and stir-fry for about 1 minute, or until the garlic shoots are tender like blanched asparagus. Taste and season with salt if necessary.

Serve immediately with steamed jasmine rice.

brussels sprouts with ginger and prawns

serves 2

Marinate the prawns in the shaoxing rice wine, pepper and sugar for 10 minutes.

Heat the oil in a wok over high heat. Add the garlic and ginger and sauté until they begin to turn golden, then add the prawns and cook for about 30 seconds until only partially cooked.

Add the Brussels sprouts and stir-fry for another 30 seconds, or just enough so there's still crunch. Stir in the fish sauce, oyster sauce, sesame oil, remaining marinade, the spring onions and the combined cornflour and water. Toss for few seconds or until the sauce thickens.

Garnish with the coriander and serve immediately with steamed jasmine rice.

LETTUCE AND GARLIC

3 tablespoons vegetable oil

3 cloves garlic, finely chopped

250g iceberg lettuce leaves, torn into quarters

1 tablespoon oyster sauce

½ teaspoon fish sauce

¼ teaspoon sugar

steamed jasmine rice, to serve

SQUID WITH BLACK BEANS AND CELERY

250g squid (or calamari), cleaned

3 tablespoons vegetable oil

2 cloves garlic, finely chopped

5–6 slices of ginger, 1–2mm thick

½–1 long red chilli, chopped

3 stalks celery, cut into 4cm pieces, sliced lengthways into 5mm batons

2 tablespoons fermented black beans (not the sauce), washed, drained and chopped roughly

1 teaspoon light soy sauce

1 tablespoon shaoxing rice wine

¼ teaspoon sesame oil

¼ teaspoon sugar

6–7 spring onions, green part only, cut into 4cm batons

steamed jasmine rice, to serve

lettuce and garlic

serves 2

Heat the oil in a wok over high heat. Sauté the garlic until it begins to turn golden. Add the lettuce, oyster sauce, fish sauce and sugar and stir-fry for about 1 minute, or until the lettuce is just wilted.

Serve immediately with rice.

squid with black beans and celery

serves 2

To prepare the squid Asian style, lie the squid or calamari tube flat on a chopping board. Slide a knife into the tube and slice through one side. Open out the tube so it sits flat with the inside facing up. Carefully score (see note below) the flesh by making diagonal slits that are about 3mm apart, then repeat on a perpendicular angle to create a lattice effect. Cut into approximately 4 x 4cm squares. Set aside.

Heat the oil in a wok on high heat. Sauté the garlic and ginger until they begin to turn golden. Add the chilli and squid or calamari to the wok and stir-fry for about 30 seconds or until the squid or calamari pieces begin to curl up. Add the celery, black beans, soy, shaoxing, sesame oil, sugar and spring onions, and toss for 10–20 seconds.

Serve immediately with steamed jasmine rice.

NOTE: To score, only slice partially into the flesh. You do need some practice with this, not scoring deep enough will not make the flesh curl and scoring too deeply will make a complete incision, so you do need to be attentive. Also, if you have the outside facing up, the squid will not attractively curl to reveal the lattice pattern, which is also done to help tenderise the flesh.

sweet things

desserts & baking

almond and lime panna cotta with lychee cream

1 cup (250ml) pouring cream

²/₃ cup (150ml) milk

zest of 1 lime (omit if pairing with lychee cream)

3g gold gelatine leaves (see note below)

100ml orzata

Lychee cream (optional)

1 cup (250ml) thickened cream

2 tablespoons icing sugar

30ml best quality lychee liquor

NOTE: Gelatine leaves come in different grades — titanium, bronze, silver, gold and platinum — depending on their strength. Platinum is the strongest.

I came up with this dessert based on the idea of using Chinese dessert flavours but interpreted in a Western way. It was inspired by almond jelly with lychees, a beautiful combination and simple dessert often found at yum cha/dim sum. I have made and tasted many panna cottas in my time and I've come to realise that the amount of gelatine required to get the panna cotta to turn out perfectly is responsible for sometimes ruining everything that is wonderful about this dessert. It's particularly horrible when you can taste the gelatine over the flavour of the panna cotta, so mine has only just enough gelatine to hold it together for scooping, and with a layer of the lychee cream sitting on top, it makes for pure unadulterated creamy indulgence. For a Chinese themed dinner, I once served this in a martini glass with a red bean and black sesame glutinous rice ball (see page 188) perched against the foot of the glass.

serves 4

Heat the cream, milk and zest (if using) in a small saucepan so it is hot but bearable to touch and definitely not boiling. This is important, as boiling will cause the mixture to separate and lose its beautifully creamy consistency. Remove from the stove.

Soak the gelatine leaves in cold water for 30 seconds, squeeze out any excess water and whisk into the hot cream and milk mixture. Run the mixture through a sieve to remove any lumps and the zest. Mix in the orzata and pour into martini glasses or bowls and refrigerate for at least 3 hours or overnight.

To make the lychee cream, whisk the cream, icing sugar and lychee liquor to emulsify. Pour over the set panna cotta and serve.

crepes

This is one of my all time favourite desserts because it's one of the first things my mum taught me how to make. In my uni days, it was pretty much the only dessert I had on offer for dinner guests. I much prefer them to your regular pancakes as I love the texture of those gorgeous folds of thin, silky crepe, made even silkier with whatever sauce you've paired them with. And in my opinion, it's a classic every cook should master. I also love them because they are so versatile in terms of what you choose to fill them with, sweet or savoury. I've given you some suggestions here to keep you going.

APPLE AND CINNAMON

8 crepes (see page 33)

1kg green apples, peeled

¼ cup (55g) caster sugar

50g unsalted butter

⅓ cup (115g) honey

pinch of salt

ground cinnamon

1–2 lemons, cut into small wedges

very vanilla ice cream (see page 199) or pouring cream or vanilla yoghurt

apple and cinnamon

I first had this dish at my friend Debbie's house over a decade ago and have been making my version of it since.

serves 4

To prepare the apples, cut them into quarters, slice seeds and ends off and further cut the wedges into 3–4 slices.

Sprinkle the sugar into a large frying pan on high heat and wait for it to begin to caramelise. When it starts to turn golden, toss the butter, apples, honey and a pinch of salt into the pan, lower to medium heat and cook until the apple reaches the desired texture. I prefer mine with a bit of crunch, so I basically wilt them then turn the heat off, but if you like your apples softer, cook them a little longer bearing in mind the residual heat will take them further still. You certainly don't want baby food mush.

Scoop a good amount of the apple mixture onto half a crepe, sprinkle with some of the cinnamon, a squeeze of lemon and fold over once.

Serve with a scoop of very vanilla ice cream or a jug of pouring cream. For breakfast, a scoop of vanilla yoghurt instead of ice cream is absolutely delicious.

MAPLE SYRUP

8 crepes (see page 33)

pure maple syrup to taste

thickened cream, very vanilla ice cream (see page 199) or vanilla yoghurt

'FETTUCCINE' SUZETTE

2 crepes (see page 33)

2 tablespoons caster sugar

1/3 cup (80ml) orange juice

zest of one orange

2 tablespoons best quality orange liquor

1 tablespoon brandy

1 tablespoon unsalted butter

2–3 strawberries diced into 5mm cubes (optional)

a few mint leaves, whole or chiffonade

pouring cream to serve

maple syrup and very vanilla ice cream

This was my one and only dessert offering in my uni days, with the cheapest maple flavoured syrup and vanilla ice cream I could find.

serves 4

Drizzle maple syrup, a dollop of cream or vanilla ice cream in the middle of the crepe, fold in half, bring in the sides and roll into parcels like a spring roll. I sometimes add chopped strawberries which give a nice tart note to contrast with the sweetness of the maple syrup.

'fettuccine' suzette

My friend Elle told me of a version of this dish she had in Italy and it seemed like the most brilliant idea, so I've just ran with it, giving it a bit of a cheeky twist.

serves 1

Roll the crepes up, then slice them into 5mm strips and carefully separate. Place the 'fettuccine' strips in a tousled nest on a serving plate. Sprinkle some chopped strawberries and a few mint leaves around or on top. Set aside.

Sprinkle the sugar into a small frying pan on a high heat (must be gas) and wait for it to partially caramelise. As it starts to turn a beautiful amber, pour in the orange juice and a pinch of the zest, followed immediately by the orange liquor and brandy.

To flame (and don't be worried – unless you've added double the amount of alcohol – your eyebrows should be safe), tilt the pan away from you, so the liquid is threatening to pour out of the frying pan. The alcohol fumes will naturally attract the flame at which point you return the pan to a flat position and allow the alcohol to cook out. The flame will die naturally. Remove from the heat and pour over the 'fettuccine'.

Serve with a jug of pouring cream.

PANDAN AND COCONUT

Pandan crepes (makes 8 crepes)

⅓ cup (60g) plain flour

2 large free-range eggs

½ cup (125ml) coconut milk

¼ cup (60ml) whole milk

pinch of salt

¼ teaspoon pandan paste

butter, softened to grease pan

Coconut filling

1 cup (45g) desiccated coconut

½ cup (125ml) coconut cream

110g dark palm sugar OR the pale
   Thai kind is also fine

generous pinch of salt

Salty coconut sauce (optional)

1 cup (250ml) coconut cream

¼ cup (55g) caster sugar

½ teaspoon salt

pandan and coconut crepes

A Malaysian favourite I've been making since I was 9. The first crepe
I ever made was one of these peculiar green ones!

serves 4

To make a pandan crepe, follow the plain crepe method (see page 33) but note
there is no melted butter or oil as there is enough oil in the coconut milk, and
the vanilla extract is replaced by the pandan paste. If the coconut milk used is
thicker than usual, you may have to thin your mixture down with more milk.

To make the coconut filling, combine all the ingredients in a small saucepan
and cook on a medium heat until the sugar has completely dissolved and the
mixture is moist and sticky without any liquid. Remove from the heat and
spread out on a plate to cool before using.

To make the salty coconut sauce, combine all the ingredients in a small
saucepan and heat until the sugar has dissolved. Set aside to cool.

To assemble the crepes, scoop 1 tablespoon of the coconut filling onto the
middle of the crepe and spread it out to an elongated shape. Then fold the
crepe in half, and fold in the sides and roll into a long parcel like a spring roll.

You may serve all the parcels on a single plate piled up on top of one another
to share or as individual serves of 2 parcels per person with 2–3 tablespoons
of salty coconut sauce drizzled over them.

grape pizza

Pizza dough

4½ cups (560g) organic plain flour

1¾ teaspoons salt

7g sachet or 1 teaspoon dry yeast

¼ cup (60ml) olive oil

1¾ cups (430ml) ice water

oil, for brushing

Topping

750g grapes (I use red and white
   for visual impact)

125g raw sugar

light olive oil, for greasing

Sweet pizzas are as much fun to make as the savoury variety. In Italy a favourite is schiacciata, a fruit pizza made with grapes, traditionally during vintage. It is one of the simplest combinations: the pizza dough and grapes combine to make a tasty and inexpensive dessert.

serves 6–8

PIZZA DOUGH

Mix all the dry ingredients in a bowl with a wooden spoon. Mix the oil and water into the flour until all of the flour is incorporated. Continue mixing until the dough is of a slightly sticky consistency and sticks a little to the bottom of the bowl, but not to the side. If the dough *is* sticking to the side of the bowl, more flour is required. If it is not sticking to the very bottom, a little water (1–2 teaspoons) should be added, but only add a little at a time. You can mix by hand or machine.

Flour the work surface, then turn out the dough. Shape the dough into a rectangle and slice into 6 pieces. Flour your hands and roll each piece into a ball, then coat the surface with oil and wrap each ball in clingfilm. These will keep in the fridge for a maximum of 3 days and about 30 days in the freezer.

Take the dough from the fridge and place on a floured surface. Stretch the dough so it is 2cm thick and 10cm in diameter, or stretch it to fit your pizza pan. The best way to stretch the dough into a circular base is to make a small circle and then toss it in the air, but if you can't handle this, a rolling pin will do the job, if not as well! If the dough is very elastic and keeps springing back to its original form, let it rest for a further 10–20 minutes to allow the gluten to relax.

TOPPING

Heat the oven to 220°C (200°C fan forced).

Wash the grapes, drain and toss with half the sugar. You can use the grapes whole if you don't mind the crunchiness but if it worries you either deseed them or use a seedless variety.

Prepare a pizza pan or similar flat tray and brush with a little light oil. Divide the dough in half and roll out one portion to fit the pizza tray. Don't worry about making a perfect circle – rough enough is good enough. Place on oiled pan.

Dot some of the grapes over the base, leaving some space between them, and sprinkle on a little more sugar.

Roll out the other portion of the dough and place it over the first, pushing down around the edge to seal it. You should now have a grape sandwich. Add more of the grapes, pushing them into the valleys formed by the grapes underneath, and sprinkle with the remaining sugar.

Bake in the oven at 220°C (or wood-fired oven if you have one) for 25–30 minutes, or until the top is caramelised and the base is brown and crisp.

— Ian Parmenter

I had the most fabulous time with Ian in Margaret River. Here we've just made pizzas (me a potato and rosemary, and Ian a grape pizza) in his gorgeous wood-fired oven. Sheer Bottled Bliss, Ian!

Antonio's recipe

pears in red wine sauce

6 ripe Williams pears, not peeled

400ml red wine

rind of 1 lemon, in thin strips

$^2/_3$ cup (145g) caster sugar

whipped cream, to serve

serves 6

Heat the oven to 200°C (190°C fan forced).

Wash and put the pears upright in a suitably sized ovenproof container. You want them to fit snugly, without too much space between them.

Bake in the oven for 30–40 minutes. Remove the pears from the oven and pour in the wine. Sprinkle over the lemon rind and most of the sugar, reserving a small amount to spoon on top of the pears. Bake for another 20 minutes, by which time the wine will have reduced and thickened a little.

Put the pears in a glass bowl, pour over the red wine syrup and chill.

Divide between 6 plates, and serve with the syrup and some whipped cream.

— *Antonio Carluccio*

baked raspberries with amaretti biscuits

3 cups (375g) fresh or frozen raspberries, or 4 not-quite-ripe peaches, halved, stone removed

4–5 tablespoons brown sugar

16 amaretti biscuits

80g good quality salted butter, cubed into 8 pieces

very vanilla ice cream (see page 199) or yoghurt, or crème Anglaise (see page 199)

The first time I had this dessert was about 5 years ago, in the Dandenongs, served to me by my beautiful friend and very brilliant cook, Kirsty. All the weekend she made me meals that I copied into my first exercise book of handwritten recipes. It is one of my most important food memories because for the first time, I realised food could be an emotional experience and hence, would have a very important place in my life. At the time I wasn't such an experienced cook, so this recipe was and still is very precious to me. It is definitely what Antonio Carluccio would classify as a MOF – minimum of fuss, maximum of flavor – also what I call a 'boy' dessert – no measuring, no whisking, no delicate baking techniques whatsoever. Guys, it's so easy, you could probably make it under the watchful gaze of a young lady you fancy and maintain relative composure!

serves 4

Heat the oven to 180°C (170°C fan forced).

Pour the raspberries into a small baking dish (around 20 x 20cm, or 15cm in diameter), or the peaches skin side down in a baking dish. Sprinkle the sugar evenly over the fruit. Using your hand, crush and sprinkle the biscuits over the raspberries, breaking any larger chunks as these will burn quickly. Distribute the butter evenly over the dish of raspberries or pop a cube of butter on each peach half. Bake for about 20 minutes.

The raspberries should be bubbling and become quite syrupy and the biscuits a dark golden brown. Some like their peaches a little firmer but I love them when they have completely collapsed into a gooey mess.

Serve hot with homemade very vanilla ice cream, yoghurt or crème Anglaise. Perfect comfort food ... mmmmm ...

sticky date pudding with butterscotch sauce

200g dates, pitted and chopped

1 cup (250ml) water

1 teaspoon bicarbonate of soda
(baking soda)

1 teaspoon finely grated fresh ginger

100g unsalted butter, softened

$^2/_3$ cup (145g) caster sugar

2 large free-range eggs

1 teaspoon vanilla bean paste or
natural vanilla extract

1$^1/_2$ cups (185g) flour, sifted

2$^1/_4$ teaspoons baking powder, sifted

Cheat's butterscotch
(makes approximately 1$^1/_4$ cups)

100g unsalted butter

1 cup (220g) brown sugar

$^1/_2$ cup (125ml) pouring cream

double cream, to serve

strawberries, to serve

serves 8–10

This is an oldie but a goodie! One of those dessert menu items that's difficult to steer away from even though you've tried it 100 times. It is my cousin Natalie's recipe but my mum suggested a teaspoon of grated ginger which makes all the difference. It is completely foolproof and super quick. Traditionally a pudding is baked in a bain-marie but this one is fuss-free, straight in the oven and always comes out deliciously moist – a definite crowd-pleaser for dinner parties.

Preheat oven to 170°C (160°C fan forced).

Line a 20cm round cake tin with baking paper. Place the dates, water and bicarbonate of soda in a small saucepan and bring to the boil. Set aside and cool.

In an electric cake mixer, cream the butter and sugar until pale and fluffy. Add the eggs one by one, beating thoroughly each time. Add the vanilla, fold in the flour and date mixture. Bake on the middle shelf for appoximately 35 minutes, or until a skewer inserted in the centre of the pudding comes out clean.

To make the butterscotch sauce, combine the butter, brown sugar and cream in a saucepan and bring to the boil. Remove from the heat and set aside until required.

Serve the pudding warm with a large spoonful of the butterscotch sauce drizzled directly onto the pudding, a dollop of double cream and strawberries on the side.

sticky marbles

These marble-sized balls of glutinous dough stuffed with different flavours are loads of fun to make. Kids love them and in fact they are one of the first things I was allowed to help with in the kitchen. The original and traditional version is called tong yuin and is served at special occasions like weddings and Chinese New Year. They are made with just the glutinous rice flour dough with no stuffing. Instead they are steeped in and eaten with a ginger and pandan sugar syrup.

If you're feeling a little intimidated by making all of my wacky five flavours, just try one flavour first. If you do make all the flavours but can't eat them straightaway, before they are boiled, freeze them on trays and then transfer them to a plastic container and keep in the freezer. This way, you can take out an assortment of flavours and boil them for a quick dessert. A word of warning, these little balls cannot be refrigerated after they are boiled as they go rock hard, so they have to be cooked and eaten on the same day.

Prepare the fillings first, then the dough and then have the coatings ready for the cooked marbles to be rolled in.

five flavours (approximately 30 balls each flavour)

Fillings for 5 flavours

1. RED BEAN OR AZUKI BEAN PASTE FILLING

½ cup red bean paste (found in Asian grocers in cans or plastic packets)

2. DURIAN FILLING

250g durian pulp (found in the freezer section of Asian grocers)

1½ tablespoons coconut cream

½ cup (115g) caster sugar

2 teaspoons cornflour

1. Red bean or azuki bean paste filling

Freeze the red bean paste. Remove from the freezer and scoop as if melon balling using a ¼-teaspoon scoop (the ones that are shaped like a half sphere), so the red bean paste forms small balls. Another way to do this is by rolling a similar amount in slightly wet hands into small marbles. Place on a tray and freeze until required.

2. Durian filling

Place the durian pulp, coconut cream and sugar in a small saucepan and cook over medium heat until the sugar dissolves. Remove a tablespoon of the mixture and emulsify it with the cornflour so it becomes a sticky paste. Stir the paste mixture into the pan and cook for about a minute, or until the mixture has thickened but not caramelised. Pour into a plastic container and freeze. Once frozen, shape into balls using the same method as the azuki bean paste but do not attempt to roll them in your hands as they will melt with your body heat. Only use a ¼-teaspoon scoop method.

3. DARK PALM SUGAR FILLING

½ cup (70g) shaved dark palm sugar (Indonesian style)

4. PEANUT FILLING

1 cup (160g) salted peanuts

⅔ cup (145g) caster sugar

½ cup peanut butter

5. BLACK SESAME FILLING

¾ cup (115g) black sesame seeds, toasted

¾ cup (170g) caster sugar

50g cold butter, diced

3. Dark palm sugar filling

Shave the palm sugar by slicing thin slivers off the block and then chop roughly. Pinch small amounts together to shape into small marbles. Freeze.

4. Peanut filling

In a food processor, blitz the peanuts and sugar until the nuts are chopped evenly. Remove ½ the mixture and set aside for coating. Add the peanut butter into the food processor and pulse until incorporated. Make sure the consistency can be pinched into small marbles that keep their shape without falling apart. If they do easily fall apart, add a couple more tablespoons of peanut butter, pulse and try shaping again. Freeze the marbles after shaping.

5. Black sesame filling

In a food processor, blitz the sesame seeds and sugar briefly. Remove half the mixture and set aside for coating. Add the butter to the remaining mix and blitz until the mixture resembles a crumble texture.

Place the mixture in a plastic container, pack down tightly and refrigerate for 2 hours. Shape into balls using a ¼-teaspoon scoop, then pinch into small marbles.

Flavour	Dough	Colouring for dough	Filling	Covering
Red bean	Water dough	pink colouring	azuki bean paste	caster sugar
Durian	Water dough	yellow colouring	durian	caster sugar
Pandan palm sugar	Coconut milk dough	pandan paste to make green	dark palm sugar	desiccated coconut
Peanut	Water dough	none	peanut	peanut crumble
Black sesame	Water dough	none	black sesame	black sesame

glutinous rice flour dough

DOUGH

makes 30 marbles

Plain (amount for 1 flavour)

This recipe makes enough for one flavour, so you will need to multiply the ingredients by five if you want to attempt all the five flavours at once.

½ cup (90g) glutinous rice flour

100ml water (room temperature is fine)

few drops red liquid food colouring

few drops yellow liquid food colouring

a good dollop of pandan paste (pandan paste from Asian grocers)

Knead flour with the water or the coconut milk until the dough comes together to form a slightly moist ball. If the dough seems a little dry, add a teaspoon of water or coconut milk and knead until incorporated. Wrap in clingfilm to keep moist.

If you are making all the flavours you will have 4 balls of water dough and 1 ball of coconut milk dough. Colour each one as they are kneaded. Use the colouring sparingly as you don't want the balls to look too lurid and unpalatable.

Coconut (amount for 1 flavour)

½ cup (90g) glutinous rice flour

100ml coconut milk

FILLING THE MARBLES

Take the fillings from the freezer one flavour at a time. When doing the durian, you do have to work fast as it melts quite quickly. To stuff the dough, pinch off a small portion of the dough, roll it roughly into a ball and then squash into a disk about 4mm thick. Place prepared filling in the centre of the disk and gather the dough so the filling is covered. Pinch away any excess dough and roll in palm of your hands until you form a perfect ball about the size of a large marble. As the balls are rolled, place them on a baking tray lined with baking paper.

COATINGS FOR THE 5 FLAVOURS

½ cup (115g) caster sugar for azuki flavour

½ cup (115g) caster sugar for durian flavour

½ cup peanut crumble

½ cup black sesame crumble

½ cup (45g) desiccated coconut with ¼ teaspoon crushed sea salt mixed in

COOKING AND COATING THE MARBLES

Fill a large pot with boiling water. Have ready a slotted spoon and a sieve resting over a bowl. So you don't get confused, cook and coat one flavour of sticky marble at a time.

Drop 5–6 marbles at a time into the boiling water. Don't attempt more as you have to quickly coat each ball immediately after cooking. When the balls are cooked they float to the top. With the slotted spoon, remove the marbles and transfer to the sieve to drain for about 5 seconds. Don't leave too long or they will get sticky and unmanageable. Roll in the appropriate coating and rest on paper towels (these will catch excess moisture from the marbles as they cool) and re-coat with appropriate coating if necessary. Arrange attractively on a plate and leave to cool completely before wrapping in clingfilm.

kuih seri muka – glutinous or sticky rice with steamed custard topping

2 cups (400g) glutinous rice, washed, soaked at least 3 hours or overnight

1⅓ cup (330ml) coconut milk

1 teaspoon salt

Custard

1½ tablespoons custard powder

2½ tablespoons cornflour

2 teaspoons rice flour

1 cup (250ml) full cream milk

¾ cup (165g) sugar

1 teaspoon vanilla bean paste or natural vanilla extract or ¼ teaspoon pandan paste if you prefer a pandan flavoured custard

1 cup (250ml) coconut cream

NOTE: Kuih cannot be refrigerated and must be eaten on the day it is made.

TIP: Be very careful – it is easy to forget that steam burns, so make sure you are always wearing oven mitts when placing things in or removing things from a steamer.

serves 6

This kuih is definitely one of my mum's specialties, and one she always gets requests for whenever she offers to bring dessert to friends' dinner parties. This year I finally learnt how to make it. If you like rice custard pudding, you'll love this Malaysian version of it with the added richness of coconut milk and delectable sticky rice.

In a wok with a domed lid or a large tall pot with a flat lid, place a metal trivet and fill with water to 2cm below the trivet. Bring to the boil. It is important that there is enough steam circulating around the top of the kuih to cook it. Watch that the water level doesn't drop and you end up burning your wok or pot. Have a boiled kettle of water nearby, so you can top up whenever required.

Line a 21–22cm springform cake tin with 2 layers of foil. Make sure there are no seams or holes in the foil or the coconut milk will seep out.

Drain the rice and mix with the coconut milk and salt. Place in the prepared tin. Jiggle the tin a bit to level out the rice and coconut milk. Steam for 30–40 minutes, or until the rice is cooked. Taste a few grains to ensure they are cooked all the way through. Remove from the heat. Grab the corners of the foil to lift the disc of cooked rice out of the tin. Oil the tin, then invert the rice disc back into the tin and discard the foil. Place a piece of clingfilm loosely over the rice, then a folded tea towel, as a heat shield. Press down on the rice to compress it slightly. Make sure the surface is as even as possible. Set aside.

To make the custard layer, combine the custard powder, cornflour, rice flour, ⅓ cup of milk, sugar and vanilla bean paste or pandan paste in a bowl and whisk until smooth. Add the remainder of the milk and whisk until combined. Pour into a small saucepan and whisk on medium heat until the mixture is a very thick paste. Add the coconut cream, stir with a wooden spoon to emulsify with the paste and cook for 3–4 minutes until it thickens again. Pour over the rice and smooth over with a spatula. Steam in the wok for 20 minutes. Don't be concerned if after steaming, the custard seems a little wobbly. When the kuih cools, the custard will set further. Cool completely, about 3–4 hours, before running a knife around the edge of the tin and releasing the kuih. With a wet knife cut into bite sized diamonds and arrange on a plate into a concentric snowflake pattern.

fried-meringue balls with pandan crème patissiere

Pandan crème patissiere

2 pandan leaves, shredded by hand into thin strips and knotted into 2 bunches or ½ teaspoon pandan paste, or 1 teaspoon vanilla bean paste

1½ cup (375ml) full cream milk

5 egg yolks

½ cup (115g) caster sugar

⅓ cup (40g) plain flour

50g unsalted butter, diced

Meringue

8 egg whites

⅓ cup (40g) plain flour, sifted

⅓ cup (40g) cornflour, sifted

4 cups (1 litre) vegetable oil

caster sugar for coating

TIP: Be creative with your fillings: grated dark chocolate, orange zest and chestnut paste for a hint of jaffa or just a piece of chocolate that will melt deliciously on frying.

serves 8

PANDAN CRÈME PATISSIERE

In a medium saucepan, bring the pandan knots and milk to the boil. If you are opting for the pandan paste, just boil the milk on its own.

Meanwhile, whisk the egg yolks, sugar and vanilla, if using, until pale, thick and fluffy. Whisk in the flour until well incorporated.

Remove the pandan knots from the milk and pour the hot milk into the yolk and sugar mixture but don't wash the saucepan. Return the mixture to the saucepan and cook over medium-high heat for about 3–4 minutes, whisking continuously, until the mixture becomes quite thick. If your custard appears to be lumpy, strain the mixture through a sieve.

Transfer the mixture to a mixing bowl and allow to cool for 5 minutes. Add the pandan paste, if using, and gradually whisk in the cubes of butter until all the butter is incorporated. Cover with clingfilm directly on the custard and cool until required. This will keep for up to a week.

MERINGUE

Using an electric mixer or whisk, beat the egg whites until stiff peaks form. Gently whisk in the flours until incorporated. Don't worry if the mixture collapses substantially.

Heat the oil so that a small dollop of the meringue mix cooks until golden in about 15 seconds.

Put 1 heaped tablespoon of meringue in a ladle and make a well in the middle, drop a heaped teaspoonful of the pandan crème patissiere into the well, spoon some meringue over the top to seal in the custard. Lower the ladle over the oil and quickly slide the meringue ball into the oil. If there is a hole in the meringue, quickly try to seal it over with some more meringue before it turns over in the oil. Cook for about 3 minutes, or until golden. You can't really overcook these but you do have to watch out for undercooking, as the meringue mixture is vile and pasty when underdone. The best way to check is to cut one open and have a taste.

To finish off, immediately roll the balls in the caster sugar.

ice creams

1 cup (250ml) full cream

1 cup (250ml) coconut cream

3 pandan leaves shredded by hand and tied into 2 bunches

4 egg yolks

130g brown sugar

130g caster sugar

1 cold avocado mashed at the last minute so it doesn't oxidize

A basic ice-cream recipe is good to learn because it is also how you make a classic crème Anglaise, a classic pouring custard to accompany all your comfort desserts. To make this recipe however, you will need to invest in an ice-cream machine.

All these ice creams serve between 6 and 8 people

Poh's 'avococo' ice cream

This recipe is a union of one of my dad's favourite drinks, a slightly strange summer drink which simply consists of blitzing fresh avocado with brown sugar, milk and ice, with a classic platform of pandan and coconut which most Malaysian desserts are built upon.

In a medium saucepan bring the cream, the coconut cream and the pandan leaves to the boil. Remove from the heat.

Meanwhile, in a medium mixing bowl, whisk the egg yolks with the sugars until pale, thick and moussey. Set aside.

Fish the pandan leaves out of the saucepan. Pour the hot cream mixture into the bowl with the egg yolks and sugar mixture and whisk. Return the mixture to the same saucepan. Place over medium heat and stir with a whisk until the mixture thickens slightly. It should not at any stage bubble or boil, as high heat will split the custard.

You can tell if the custard is just right by dipping a wooden spoon into the mixture. Turn the back of the spoon towards you, and with a finger, wipe across the bottom half to remove the custard. The consistency should be like pouring cream, so it will take a moment for drips to form from the half-way line. If the custard runs down immediately, you need to return it to the heat to cook a little longer. Return the pandan leaves to the mixture to further infuse. Cover with clingfilm and refrigerate overnight or until the custard is completely chilled.

Take the pandan leaves out of the mixture and whisk in the avocado. Strain through a sieve to remove any lumps. Churn in an ice-cream machine following the manufacturer's instructions. Place in containers and freeze.

Crème Anglaise

1 cup (250ml) full cream

1 cup (250ml) full cream milk

4 egg yolks

250g caster sugar

2 teaspoons vanilla bean paste

very vanilla

This is the most useful ice cream recipe of all. With it under your belt, the possibilities are endless and you can go off to create your own unique flavours.

To make the crème Anglaise, in a medium saucepan bring the cream and the milk to the boil. Remove from the heat.

Meanwhile in a bowl, whisk the egg yolks, caster sugar and vanilla bean paste until pale, thick and moussey. Pour the hot cream and milk into the egg mixture. Whisk briefly to incorporate the two mixtures and then return to the saucepan. Whisk gently over low-medium heat, until the mixture thickens slightly. It should not at any point bubble or boil, as high heat will split the custard.

You can tell if the custard is just right by dipping a wooden spoon into the mixture. Turn the back of the spoon towards you, and with a finger, wipe across the bottom half to remove the custard. The consistency should be like pouring cream, so it will take a moment for drips to form from the half-way line. If the custard runs down immediately, you need to return the custard to the heat to cook a little longer. At this point you have a crème Anglaise to serve warm or chilled.

Refrigerate overnight or until completely chilled. Churn in an ice-cream machine. Place in containers and freeze.

Crème Anglaise

1 cup (250ml) full cream

1 cup (250ml) full cream milk

4 egg yolks

270g caster sugar

1 teaspoon vanilla bean paste

1 cup fresh strawbery, mango, passionfruit or raspberry puree, chilled

strawberry, mango, passionfruit or raspberry

Make the crème Anglaise, following the very vanilla method but with chilled fruit puree of your choice. You will also notice the amount of caster sugar is increased to 270g to counteract the acid in the fruit.

For a more refined ice cream, you may want to run the puree through a sieve to catch any seeds or fibres, before adding to the crème Anglaise.

If you want to create a ripple effect like the one in the photo, fold your fruit puree through the crème Anglaise immediately after churning and then freeze.

Crème Anglaise

1 cup (250ml) full cream

1 cup (250ml) full cream milk

4 egg yolks

250g caster sugar

2 teaspoons vanilla bean paste

1 quantity praline

Praline

1 cup (155g) almonds, roasted

½ cup (125ml) hot water

¾ cup (170g) caster sugar

almond praline

Make the crème Anglaise, following the very vanilla ice cream recipe but mix crushed almond praline into the churned crème Anglaise before freezing.

To make the praline, heat the oven to 180°C (170°C fan forced). Roast the almonds for 7–10 minutes on a baking tray. Taste one – if they aren't roasted enough, and still tasting a little raw and green, return to the oven for another 4–5 minutes. Tip the almonds out, grease the tray lightly with butter and return almonds to the tray. Set aside.

Combine the water and the sugar in a small saucepan and stir until the sugar is dissolved. Crank up the heat so it boils but PLEASE don't stir as this will cause the sugar to crystallise and refuse to caramelise (unfortunately, there's no going back when this happens – you just have to start from scratch).

Now, this is where you have to be brave and justifiably a bit edgy. Take the caramel as 'far' as you can without it suddenly, and I stress 'suddenly', going from dreamy golden, to black and smoking – it literally happens within the blink of an eye, and I'm afraid the only way to get good at this, is by experience. Just remember that the caramel keeps cooking feverishly even when you remove it from the heat. To caramelise generally takes about 10 minutes.

Now, when your caramel is a beautiful dark amber, immediately tip it over the roasted almonds. Roll the caramel around so it spreads evenly over the almonds and allow it to cool but be warned the caramel is very hot and will instantly conduct intense heat through the metal tray, so remember to use oven mitts.

When completely cool, it will be solid and brittle. Remove the praline disk from the tin by smashing the tin down on the bench top, and peel off the baking paper. Put the praline disk into a mortar and pestle and break it into small pieces or chop it finely. You can also place the praline in a plastic bag and take your frustrations out on it with a rolling pin! Cool shattered praline further in the fridge or freezer before combining with the churned very vanilla.

Crème Anglaise

1 cup (250ml) full cream

1 cup (250ml) full cream milk

4 egg yolks

150g caster sugar

2 teaspoons vanilla bean paste

Butterscotch

1 quantity butterscotch sauce
    (see page 204)

butterscotch

Make the crème Anglaise, following the very vanilla ice cream method but note the sugar has been reduced because of the additional sugar content in the butterscotch sauce. Make the butterscotch sauce, chill and then add it to the crème Anglaise.

If you want butterscotch ripple, add only half the butterscotch to the crème Anglaise. After the ice cream has been churned, fold in the remaining butterscotch then scoop into containers and freeze.

Crème Anglaise

1 cup (250ml) full cream

1 cup (250ml) full cream milk

4 egg yolks

110g caster sugar

2 teaspoons vanilla bean paste

Choc hazelnut

$\frac{1}{3}$ cup chocolate hazelnut spread

$\frac{1}{2}$ cup crushed roasted hazelnuts

choc hazelnut

Make the crème Anglaise, following the very vanilla method but note the sugar has been reduced because of the additional sugar content in the hazelnut spread. While the crème Anglaise is still hot, add the chocolate hazelnut spread, and if you want some texture, add crushed roasted hazelnuts to the crème Anglaise just before churning.

To roast the hazelnuts, set oven at 180°C. Place the nuts on a baking tray and bake for about 7–10 minutes or until the skins split and start to flake off. Remove from the oven, pour the hazelnuts onto a clean tea towel. Using the tea towel to shield your hands from the heat, rub until all the skin flake off. It's perfectly fine if not all of the skins will rub off. Turn your knife on its side so it is parallel with the chopping board to split the nuts in half, so they don't roll madly around (a tip from Emmanuel), and chop to the desired consistency. Cool the nuts completely in the fridge before adding to the chilled crème Anglaise.

orange chiffon cake

5 egg whites (at room temperature)

½ teaspoon cream of tartar, sifted

⅓ cup (75g) caster sugar

5 egg yolks

⅓ cup (75g) caster sugar, extra

5 tablespoons (100ml) coconut milk

4 tablespoons (80ml) vegetable oil

4 tablespoons (80ml) orange juice

1 tablespoon finely grated orange zest

150 plain flour, sifted

1¾ teaspoons baking powder, sifted

pinch of salt

Roasted hazelnuts

150g hazelnuts

This is an old Malaysian favourite but I have recently found out it was invented in the late 1920s by a Californian insurance salesman turned caterer! Interestingly, it has become very popular in Asia where in the past, dairy has been scarce and the fat content is replaced by oil and the cake eaten without any further dressing. You will note an interesting feature in the method that specifies using a tin which is NOT non-stick and further, not to grease it. The reason for this is that to achieve the impressive height and lightness of a classic chiffon cake, you are essentially attempting to defy gravity. By immediately inverting it as it comes out of the oven, the 'stick' factor keeps the cake suspended and the cake from collapsing. You will see how easy it is to be creative once you've mastered the basic recipe. Here, I'm showing you 4 different cakes that use the same basic recipe, which was given to me by my close friend Betty Lee.

serves 8-10

Preheat the oven to 170° (160°C fan forced).

In a large bowl, beat the egg whites and cream of tartar with an electric mixer until soft peaks form. Add the sugar 1 tablespoon at a time and beat thoroughly after each addition until you achieve stiff peaks. Set aside.

In a separate bowl, whisk the egg yolks with the extra caster sugar until thick, pale and fluffy. Add coconut milk, vegetable oil, orange juice and zest, flour and baking powder, and whisk until combined. Gently fold (see note on page 210) the egg whites into the yolk mixture in 3 batches.

Pour into a 22cm angel cake tin (see note). It is important that you do not use a non-stick tin and do not grease it. Bake for 30 minutes on the middle shelf, or until a skewer inserted in the centre of the cake comes out clean. Leave the oven on for roasting the hazelnuts.

When the cake is out of the oven, immediately invert the tin and leave the cake in the tin to cool completely (about 2 hours).

ROASTED HAZELNUTS

Place the hazelnuts on a baking tray and roast for 7 minutes, or until the skins are splitting and flakey. Remove from the oven and pour into the middle of a clean tea towel, wrap up and gently rub the skins off. Place the nuts on a chopping board and chop to desired texture.

....

NOTE: An angel cake tin is a special ring tin with a removable flat bottom, and flat, not fluted, sides.

....

Filling

400ml pouring cream

3 tablespoons icing sugar

1 teaspoon vanilla bean paste or
natural vanilla extract

Ganache

150ml pouring cream

200g good quality dark chocolate,
finely chopped

Butterscotch

1/2 cup (125ml) hot water

1 1/2 cups (345g) caster sugar

1 cup (250ml) full cream

Filling and icing

600ml full cream

1 teaspoon vanilla bean paste or
natural vanilla extract

1/3 cup (40g) pure icing sugar

2 punnets strawberries, diced into
5mm cubes, leave 8 whole to
decorate

FILLING

Whip the cream, sugar and vanilla in a bowl until stiff, be careful not to overbeat as the cream will split. Cover with clingfilm and refrigerate until required.

When the cake is cool and ready to be assembled, run a knife around the edge and base of the cake and invert to release. Slice the cake with a sharp chef's knife into 3 equal layers. Spread half of the filling and a third of the chopped hazelnuts on each layer.

GANACHE

Bring the cream to the boil in a small saucepan. Remove from the heat, add chocolate and whisk until the chocolate is melted and well combined. Place the cake on a wire rack and, using a spatula, spread the ganache evenly over the top and side of the cake and sprinkle with the remaining chopped hazelnuts.

strawberry and butterscotch chiffon cake

Use the orange chiffon cake recipe and method but replace the orange juice and zest with 1 1/2 teaspoons of vanilla bean paste or natural vanilla extract and use only 2 1/2 tablespoons (50ml) of vegetable oil.

To make the butterscotch, combine the water and sugar in a medium saucepan over high heat and stir until the sugar is dissolved. Crank up the heat so it boils. PLEASE don't stir as this will cause the sugar to crystallise and it will refuse to caramelise (unfortunately, there's no going back when this happens, you just have to start from scratch). Now, this is where you have to be brave. Take the caramel as 'far' as you can without it suddenly, and I stress 'suddenly', going from dreamy golden, to black and smoking – it happens within the blink of an eye, literally; and I'm afraid the only way to get good at this, is through experience. It generally takes about 10 minutes, but just remember that the caramel keeps cooking feverishly even when you remove it from the heat. (So if you are a novice at this, err on the side of a paler caramel.) Now, when this magical window of time happens and your caramel is a beautiful dark amber, remove it from the heat and whisk in the cream; it may splatter, so beware. If the mixture goes a little lumpy, return to the heat and whisk for a few seconds. Remove from the heat and cool until required.

To make icing, whip the cream, sugar and vanilla until stiff but do not overbeat as the cream will split and become unmanageable. The texture to look for is one you can slice through with a knife and the cut not collapse in on itself. Cover with clingfilm and refrigerate until required.

When the cake is cool and ready to be assembled, run a knife around both the outside and inside edges and the bottom of the tin and invert. Slice the cake with a sharp chef's knife into 3 equal layers. Spread ¾ cup of the icing mixture, half the chopped strawberries, then ½ the butterscotch on each layer. To finish off, use a spatula or butter knife to spread the entire surface of the cake with the remaining icing. Garnish with whole strawberries.

1 tablespoon instant expresso coffee powder

1 teaspoon vanilla bean paste or natural vanilla extract

Filling and icing

600ml full cream

1 teaspoon vanilla bean paste or natural vanilla extract

⅓ cup (40g) pure icing sugar

3-4 ripe bananas, thinly sliced

200g good quality dark chocolate, finely grated, for sprinkling

PANDAN CHIFFON CAKE

10 egg whites (at room temperature)

1 teaspoon cream of tartar, sifted

⅔ cup (145g) caster sugar

10 egg yolks

10½ tablespoons (210ml) coconut milk

4½ tablespoons (90ml) vegetable oil

⅔ (145g) caster sugar

1 teaspoon pandan paste

300g plain flour, sifted

3½ teaspoons baking powder, sifted

pinch of salt

banoffee chiffon cake with choc chip icing

Use the orange chiffon cake recipe and method but replace the orange juice and zest with 1 heaped tablespoon of sifted instant espresso coffee powder and 1 teaspoon of vanilla bean paste or natural vanilla extract and only 2½ tablespoons (50ml) of vegetable oil.

You may also add the butterscotch sauce from the previous recipe to this if you want to have another layer of indulgence.

To make the icing and filling, whip the cream, vanilla and sugar in a bowl until stiff, be careful not to overbeat as the cream will split. Cover with clingfilm and refrigerate until required.

When the cake is cool and ready to be assembled, run a knife around the edge of the cake then invert the tin on to a wire rack to release. Slice the cake with a large sharp chef's knife into 3 equal layers. Spread each layer with ¾ cup of the cream mixture, half the sliced banana and ½ of the butterscotch (if using). Mix the remaining cream with the grated chocolate and using a spatula or a butter knife, spread evenly over the entire surface of the cake.

pandan chiffon cake

The method for this is the same as the orange chiffon except you replace the orange juice and zest with the pandan paste and less vegetable oil is used. The quantities are also doubled. This is because a pandan chiffon is eaten plain, with no dressing whatsoever, so you need more batter to achieve the signature height of a classic chiffon cake.

fudgey pink forest cake with choc-chip icing

220g unsalted butter, softened

350g brown sugar

1 teaspoon vanilla bean paste or natural vanilla extract

2 large free-range eggs

100g dark chocolate, melted (for details about melting chocolate see page 227 of the Glossary)

200g plain flour, sifted

1 cup (250ml) boiling water (if you wish, dissolve 1 tablespoon instant coffee powder in this for a mocha flavour)

1 teaspoon bicarbonate of soda, sifted

Crème Chantilly

3 cups (750ml) full cream

1/2 cup (115g) icing sugar

2 teaspoons vanilla bean paste or natural vanilla extract

Icing and filling

100g dark chocolate, coarsely grated

few drops of red food colouring (optional)

3/4 cup (180ml) kirsch liqueur

700g bottle of morello cherries, drained

10 maraschino cherries with stems, drained and dried on paper towel

This black forest recipe has evolved from the magic chocolate cake I've been making for years. Its texture is more substantial to that of a regular black forest but it hits all the same notes – a fab one for birthdays.

serves 10

Set oven to 170°C/160°C fan forced. Line a 20–21cm round cake tin with baking paper.

Using an electric cake mixer, cream the butter, sugar and vanilla until pale and fluffy. Add the eggs, one at a time beating thoroughly after each. Swap to a whisk and whisk in the melted chocolate until thoroughly incorporated. Whisk in 1/4 of the flour, then 1/4 cup of water and all of the bicarbonate of soda. Alternate whisking in the flour and water until all are incorporated.

Pour the batter into the prepared tin and bake on the middle shelf for 1 hour or until an inserted skewer comes out clean. Cool for 3 hours in the tin before icing.

To make the crème Chantilly, whip the cream with the icing sugar and vanilla with an electric beater or a whisk until it is very stiff, but be careful not to split the cream. Transfer 2 2/3 cups into another mixing bowl, cover with clingfilm and refrigerate. To make choc-chip icing, mix the remaining crème Chantilly, grated dark chocolate and food colouring thoroughly with a spoon. Cover with clingfilm and refrigerate.

To ice the cake, invert it on the kitchen bench and slice it into 3 equal layers. Carefully lift off the top 2 layers. Starting with the bottom layer, spoon 4 tablespoons of kirsch over the entire surface, then spread 3/4 cup of the plain crème Chantilly right to the edges of the cake. Divide the morello cherries in half and distribute equally one half over the top of the cream. Repeat the process for the second layer. Spoon the remaining kirsch over the top of the cake. Press the cake down gently to make sure the layers are secure.

Slather all the choc-chip icing on the entire cake and smooth over. With the remaining plain crème Chantilly, fill a piping bag with a fluted nozzle and pipe 10 rosettes around the edge of the cake and, for a nicer finish, a scallop pattern along the bottom. To finish, pop a maraschino cherry on top of each rosette. There you have it – Fudgey Pink Forest Cake!

the best banana cake in the world

Cake

125g unsalted butter, softened

$\frac{1}{2}$ cup (115g) brown sugar, firmly pressed down

$\frac{1}{2}$ cup (115g) caster sugar

1 teaspoon vanilla bean paste or natural vanilla extract

2 large free-range eggs

1$\frac{1}{2}$ cups (185g) plain flour, sifted

2$\frac{1}{4}$ teaspoons baking powder, sifted

$\frac{1}{2}$ teaspoon bicarbonate of soda (baking soda), sifted

$\frac{1}{4}$ teaspoon salt

$\frac{1}{4}$ cup (60ml) full cream milk

3 overripe bananas, mashed

Icing

50g good quality salted butter, softened

$\frac{1}{2}$ cup (60g) icing sugar

2–3 tablespoons lemon or lime juice

$\frac{1}{4}$ cup (35g) roasted hazelnuts, chopped (see page 201 for how to roast hazelnuts)

This is the fluffiest, most moist banana cake you'll ever taste. Paired with lemon icing and a sprinkle of chopped hazelnuts, I'm convinced it's the best banana cake in the world!

Preheat the oven to 160° C (150°C fan forced). Line a 20cm round cake tin with baking paper or grease and flour your tin.

With an electric mixer, cream the butter, both sugars and vanilla until pale and fluffy. Add 1 egg at a time, mixing thoroughly each time. Add the flour, baking powder, bicarbonate of soda and salt, and fold in with a wooden spoon until fully incorporated. Add the milk and banana, and fold in (see note below). Pour the batter into the prepared tin and bake on the middle shelf for about 40 minutes, or until a skewer inserted in the centre of the cake comes out clean. Allow to cool for 5–10 minutes before running a knife around the tin to release. Cool on a wire rack. If you have used baking paper for the base and sides of the tin, the cake will easily fall out.

To make the icing, combine butter, the sugar and lemon juice in a bowl and beat with an electric mixer until pale and fluffy. Spread over the top of the cake (it won't seem much, but it is the perfect amount) and sprinkle with the hazelnuts. YUM!

NOTE: In cooking terms, 'folding' is a method of delicately mixing one ingredient, usually flour or beaten egg whites, into a batter. The action involves turning the bowl with one hand and with the other, scraping the sides and bottom of the mixing bowl and draping whatever is collected along the way over the surface of the mixture. It is usually an action performed with a thin implement, so it effectively 'cuts' through the mixture nicely without destroying any aeration previously created but still amalgamating the ingredients.

TIP: If you find yourself without any baking paper, brush the entire inside of your cake tin with melted butter, wipe out any excess with a paper towel. Sprinkle 3 tablespoons of plain flour into the tin and rotate the tin so the flour sticks to the butter. Tap the sides continually to release any excess flour, making sure every part of the tin is coated. Discard any excess flour.

chocolate éclairs

Choux pastry

¾ cup (190ml) full cream milk

90g unsalted butter, finely diced

1 teaspoon salt

1 teaspoon sugar

¾ cup (90g) plain flour, sifted

3 large free-range eggs, lightly beaten

Chocolate cream

¾ cup (190ml) pouring cream

½ cup (125ml) milk

4 egg yolks

¼ cup (55g) caster sugar

16g dark chocolate (70 per cent cocoa), chopped

Fondant chocolate icing

200g soft white fondant (available from gourmet food stores)

30g cocoa powder

water

makes 10

Heat the oven to 180°C if using gas or 200°C fan forced and line a baking tray with baking paper.

In a saucepan, combine the milk, butter, salt and sugar and bring to the boil. Remove from the heat, add the flour and mix well with a wooden spoon. Put the saucepan back on medium heat and cook the dough for 3–5 minutes, or until it resembles a ball.

Transfer the dough to a bowl. Add the eggs, one by one, mixing well each time. The pastry can be used straight away or left to rest for up to 40 minutes, covered with clingfilm.

Put some of the choux pastry into a piping bag (do not overfill) with a 1.5cm nozzle and pipe out ten 12cm long sausages onto the tray. Leave plenty of space around each one so they won't touch during baking.

Bake for 30 minutes, then reduce the oven temperature to 150°C (140°C fan forced) and bake for a further 15 minutes. Do not open the oven during cooking or the pastry will collapse. Transfer the éclairs to a wire rack to cool.

Fill the éclairs with chocolate cream by making a hole in the bottom of one end and piping with an 8mm nozzle (size 6). Top with fondant chocolate icing.

CHOCOLATE CREAM

Put the cream and the milk in a saucepan and bring to the boil. Whisk the egg yolks and sugar in a large bowl until thick and pale. Add the hot cream mixture and cook over low heat for 5–6 minutes, stirring constantly, without boiling, until the mixture thickens and coats the back of a spoon. Take it off the heat and stir in the chocolate to melt. Let it cool, and refrigerate overnight.

FONDANT CHOCOLATE ICING

Melt the white fondant in the microwave for 20 seconds; it should not be too hot. Add the cocoa, more if you want a stronger chocolate flavour, and water if necessary to make a consistency soft enough for dipping the eclairs in. Immediately dip the tops of the éclairs into the fondant, allowing any excess to drip down the sides, and place on a wire rack to set.

— *Emmanuel Mollois*

215

macaroons

Macaroons

280g very fine almond meal

480g icing sugar

7 egg whites (see note below) (separated for 4 days and kept in fridge if the weather is hot)

For chocolate macaroons

2 teaspoons best quality cocoa powder, sifted

For pineapple/avocado macaroons

Light green food colouring

Butter cream

250g butter, softened out of the fridge overnight

1 large free-range egg

2 egg yolks

100g sugar

25ml water

....

NOTE: Use 50g eggs to achieve the right proportions.

....

A choice of two colourful macaroons: chocolate, or pineapple and avocado, which gives a light green colour. Because you have to let the butter cream filling cool and set, I suggest you make the fillings first then the macaroons.

makes 65

MACAROONS

Pass the almond meal, sugar and cocoa, if making chocolate macaroons, twice through a very fine sieve.

Meanwhile, in a large bowl, beat the egg whites until stiff. Fold in the almond and sugar mixture (add the green colouring at this stage if making pineapple/avocado macaroons). Rest the mixture for 10 minutes – this helps it to relax, and slightly thicken.

Line a baking tray with baking paper, and place it on top of another tray. This is to make sure the macaroons do not cook too quickly or burn. Using a piping bag with a 5mm plain nozzle, pipe 3.5cm rounds onto the lined tray. Leave a 4cm space between each macaroon to allow for spreading.

Stand for 25–30 minutes – this will allow them to 'crouter', form a crust.

Meanwhile heat the oven to 200°C for a non fan-forced oven but to 230°C for a fan-forced oven (a fan-forced oven cools more quickly than an ordinary oven). Place the macaroons in the oven, immediately reduce the temperature to 140°C (130°C fan forced) and cook for 25 minutes, or until the tops of the macaroons are dry but not coloured.

Remove from the oven and allow to cool on the trays completely. Voila ...

BUTTER CREAM

In an electric mixer, beat the egg and the egg yolks on speed 1. Continue beating the eggs while you make the sugar syrup. In a small saucepan heat the sugar and water until it reaches 121°C (you will need a sugar thermometer). Turn the beating eggs up to the top speed, and slowly add the sugar syrup. Continue beating until the mixture completely cools. Keep beating and slowly add the butter bit by bit until it is well combined and shiny.

PINEAPPLE AND AVOCADO MACAROONS

1 quantity macaroons

1 quantity butter cream

1 quantity white chocolate ganache

1 quantity pineapple avocado coulis

White chocolate ganache

300g white chocolate, roughly chopped

½ cup (125ml) pouring cream

Pineapple and avocado coulis

½ small pineapple, peeled, cored and finely diced

1 ripe avocado, diced

125g caster sugar

1 vanilla bean, cut in half lengthways and seeds scraped

½ teaspoon ground Szechuan pepper

CHOCOLATE MACAROONS

1 quantity chocolate macaroons

1 quantity butter cream

1 quantity dark chocolate ganache

Dark chocolate ganache

1 cup (250ml) pouring cream

250g roughly chopped dark chocolate, 70 per cent cocoa

pineapple and avocado macaroon filling

The macaroon biscuit is filled with a combination of white chocolate ganache, coulis and butter cream.

To make the white chocolate ganache, melt the white chocolate in the microwave. Bring the cream to the boil and then add to the melted chocolate and mix with a wooden spoon. Alternatively, melt the chocolate in a heatproof bowl placed over a saucepan of simmering water, and then add the boiling cream.

To make the coulis, place all the ingredients in a saucepan, cook over medium heat for 5 minutes, or until softened. Place in a blender or food processor and blend until smooth. Push through a sieve and discard any pulp. Chill.

Combine the ganache, coulis, and butter cream and stir well until combined. To fill the macaroons, dollop a generous amount of filling onto the flat side of a macaroon, sandwich with another and press tightly together.

chocolate macaroon filling

To make the dark chocolate ganache, put the chocolate in a large bowl. Bring the cream to the boil, add to the chocolate and mix with a wooden spoon. Allow to chill, to thicken.

Stir the chocolate ganache and butter cream together (they must be at the sauce temperature) until well combined. To fill the macaroons, dollop a generous amount of filling onto the flat side of a macaroon, sandwich with another and press tightly together.

— *Emmanuel Mollois*

LYCHEE MACAROON FILLING

pink food colouring, liquid or powdered

beetroot powder (available at gourmet shops but optional)

Filling

250g unsalted butter

200g icing sugar

$\frac{1}{4}$ cup best quality lychee liquor

7 lychees (from a tin), pureed

....

NOTE: Make sure you do have lots of baking trays ready – the mixture needs to be piped in one hit as it doesn't sit well in the mixing bowl. You also need time for the piped mixture to form a crust and this may vary depending on the weather.

....

Poh's lychee macaroons

This lychee macaroon came about as a challenge from Emmanuel and of course I had to add an oriental twist with a peppering of colour. The vibrant red skin of the lychee is what inspired me to use beetroot powder. I thought it would be a rare opportunity to play with an intense colour because we were using a natural dye. Sadly, as Emmanuel had warned, the colour completely dissipates to a pale burnt orange on high temperatures. It still looked very pretty but not the right colour to evoke the flavour of lychee. I was determined to use the stuff though, so a sprinkle of beetroot powder on a pale pink macaroon, it was!

Follow Emmanuel's macaroon recipe (see page 215), except where Emmanuel uses green food colouring, replace with red and a sprinkle of the beetroot powder.

To make the filling, beat the butter with the icing sugar until very pale and fluffy. Add the lychee liquor in 2 batches and hand whisk to emulsify. Add lychee puree and hand whisk until incorporated. If the mixture seems a little curdley, do not be concerned. I've made this several times and it won't separate.

To assemble, using a piping bag with a 5mm nozzle, pipe a dollop of lychee butter cream in the middle of the underside of a macaroon and sandwich another on top. Press gently together so the cream oozes towards the edge. Refrigerate before serving. Store in an airtight container with sheets of plastic or baking paper between each layer, in the fridge or freezer for up to 2 weeks.

chewy choc-chip and macadamia cookies

170g unsalted butter, softened

220g tightly packed brown sugar

1 tablespoon natural vanilla extract

2 large free-range eggs

1⅔ cup (210g) plain flour, sifted

½ teaspoon baking powder, sifted

½ teaspoon salt

200g dark or milk chocolate, roughly chopped

1 cup (160g) macadamias or your choice of nut, chopped roughly

Whoever first said 'a balanced diet is a cookie in each hand' was inspired. For years I've been trying to find a good recipe for this classic American cookie. After experimenting with several that I found on the internet, I came up with this, and they're so dangerously moreish, I recommend doubling the recipe every time. Otherwise, they seem to disappear before they've done their stint on the cooling rack, especially if there are sneaky little fingers in the house!

makes 20–22

Heat the oven to 170°C (160°C fan forced).

With an electric mixer, cream the butter, sugar and vanilla until pale and fluffy. Add the eggs, one at a time, mixing thoroughly each time. Add the flour and baking powder and mix with a wooden spoon or spatula until incorporated. Tip in the chocolate and macadamias and mix until evenly dispersed through the dough.

Line 2 baking trays with baking paper and dollop ¼ cups of cookie dough spaced 5cm apart. Bake on the middle shelf for 15 minutes, or until the cookies are a pale gold around the edges. If you over cook these, they will still be delicious but they will lose their lovely chewiness and you will have a crispy cookie instead. Remove from the oven and allow to rest on the trays for 5 minutes before transferring to a wire rack. Store in an airtight container if they last that long!

melting moments

Shortbread

250g good quality salted butter, soft

⅓ cup (40g) icing sugar, plus extra for dusting

1 teaspoon natural vanilla extract

1½ cups (185g) plain flour

½ cup (65g) cornflour

glazed red cherries, cut into 5mm pieces (omit if sandwiching with lemon curd)

Lazy lemon curd (makes 600ml)

1 teaspoon finely grated lemon zest

⅔ cup (160ml) lemon juice

1⅓ cups (310g) caster sugar

250g unsalted butter, diced

4 large free-range eggs, lightly beaten

pinch of salt

TIP: If you don't have a piping bag use 2 spoons to shape the batter into roundish dollops. It won't look as pretty but it will taste just as yum.

I've been making these dainty little shortbreads as Christmas gifts for my extended family since I was 9, so after 26 years, I think I can claim it's a tradition! It's one of the first things my mum taught me to make, so I have lovely memories of learning to cook whenever I bake them every year. They're incredibly moreish and I have to say my family absolutely loves them, although the packages are shrinking each year as I get older and busier.

Now, melting moments are traditionally teamed up with a lemon cream in the middle and even though I've always served them plain, I'm thinking a lemon curd would make a lovely pairing for a gift, jarred and wrapped with a bit of ribbon. The curd will not last unrefrigerated, so only sandwich with the biscuit as you need them.

makes about 40 individual biscuits

Heat the oven to 170°C (160°C fan forced).

Line a baking tray with baking paper.

With an electric mixer, cream the butter and sugar until pale and fluffy. Add the vanilla and beat briefly. Stir in the flour, cornflour and salt. Spoon the mixture into a piping bag fitted with a fluted nozzle and pipe 3cm rosettes onto the prepared tray lined with baking paper. Leave a 2cm space between each rosette. Top each rosette with a piece of glazed cherry and bake for 10-15 minutes, or until golden. Cool on a wire rack.

When cool, lightly dust with the extra icing sugar. Handle gently when storing as they are very short and crumble easily.

To make the lemon curd, bung all the ingredients in a saucepan over medium heat and stir with a wooden spoon or whisk until thickened. Strain, cover with clingfilm and chill until thickened. This will make more than you need but it will keep for 2 weeks in the fridge, and is delicious on toast. Easy!

cherry and hazelnut friands

½ cup (60g) plain flour

1½ cups (185g) icing sugar, sifted

1 teaspoon ground cinnamon

1 cup (110g) hazelnut or almond meal

180g unsalted butter, melted

6 egg whites, lightly beaten

400g bottled morello cherries, drained, or any other fruit (I like raspberries and green apples)

I've never fancied cupcakes. I've always found them somewhat shallow and fussy. The first time I tasted one of these, however, I thought, wow – so much more substantial in flavour and texture – this is where it's at. To top it off, the method is incredibly simple: a muffin method using melted butter and all the ingredients in together for a quick whisk and you're there. This delicious rendition using sour cherries is from one of my mum's friends, Christina. To serve it as a dessert, she reserves the cherry juice, thickens it with a sprinkle of cornflour (you could add a kiss of hazelnut liquor or kirsch for a bit of cheekiness) and serves the friands in a glossy pool of it. Perhaps a dollop of double cream as well. Please do not throw away the leftover egg yolks as you can make pasta, custard or ice cream with them! Never waste anything.

makes 12

Preheat the oven to 170°C (160°C fan forced).

Line a standard 12-hole muffin pan with paper cases or grease a 12-hole friand tin with melted butter.

Combine all the ingredients in a large bowl, except the cherries, and stir with a whisk until there are no lumps.

Distribute the batter into the paper cases or friand tin. Then poke 4–5 cherries (or whatever fruit you've chosen) into each friand so they are covered by batter. Bake on the middle shelf for about 15 minutes, or until a skewer inserted in the centre of a friand comes out clean. If using a friand mould, leave to cool for 5–10 minutes before turning out onto a cooling rack.

TIP: If you'd like to add a bit of texture, you may sprinkle some chopped hazelnuts over the top before baking.

suji biscuits

230g ghee

150g caster or icing sugar (icing sugar creates a shorter texture than caster)

1 teaspoon natural vanilla extract or almond essence

300g plain flour, sifted

1 teaspoon baking powder, sifted

1 cup (100g) almond meal

red glazed cherries, cut into tiny pieces for decoration

Suji or sugee biscuits are East Indian by origin and, like a lot of Indian sweets, are traditionally made with semolina. I was doing some research on almonds for an episode of the show and found out that for these particular biscuits, it's quite common to substitute almond meal for the semolina. The result is a most gorgeously flavoured marzipan biscuit short as short can be! Very moreish. But super delicate, so please handle with care. They practically crumble if you stare at them too hard!

makes approximately 40 biscuits

Preheat the oven to 160°C (150°C fan forced). Line a baking tray with baking paper.

With an electric cake mixer, cream the ghee, sugar and vanilla or almond essence until pale and fluffy. Add the flour and baking powder and mix with a wooden spoon. Add the almond meal and mix until combined.

Roll the dough into balls the size of large marbles. Place on the prepared tray about 2cm apart. If your hands get very sticky, just wash and moisten slightly before continuing to roll. Top with a piece of cherry and squash down a little.

Bake for 10–12 minutes, or until pale gold – these are not meant to be golden brown. Cool on a wire rack and store in an airtight container.

TIP: Omitting the baking powder will result in a slightly more dense texture.

glossary

2

1

3

INGREDIENTS

Assam, see tamarind.

Atta flour (2) is unprocessed flour used in Indian cooking mostly to make unleavened types of bread. It is similar to wholemeal flour but without the husk and therefore more gentle on the digestion. It imparts a subtle nutty flavor.

Soft bean curd skins (3) are the soft pliable skins most commonly used for wrapping a range of fillings to form dumplings. Resembling sheets of wrinkled, golden paper, they can be found in Chinese grocers, folded flat in plastic packaging. There are many types of bean curd skins available. When purchasing, ensure that you can bend the package without shattering the skins as this will let you know you have chosen the right sort.

Belachan (4a) is a pungent, dark brown, sun dried, fermented shrimp paste. Different varieties exist, including a dark Indonesian version, a lighter one from Melaka, Malaysia, and a slightly different Thai form called gapi (see below). Belachan is used in small amounts, toasted and crumbled, in salads, relishes, soups and curries. Used widely throughout Southeast Asia, it is available in paste, powder or cake form.

Cardamom (32c, d and f) is closely related to ginger and is native to India. Found commonly in Indian food, its use is now widespread for culinary and medicinal purposes. The most common types of cardamom pods are green **(32d)** and black **(32f)** (sometimes called brown). Thai cardamom is milder than green cardamom, and has a delicate flavour.

Chinese chives (5b) (see garlic chives)

Chinese preserved shredded olives (6) are almost black in appearance, salted and preserved in oil. You will find them in jars, available from Asian grocers and most commonly used as a condiment on rice congee or in stir-fries.

4

6

5

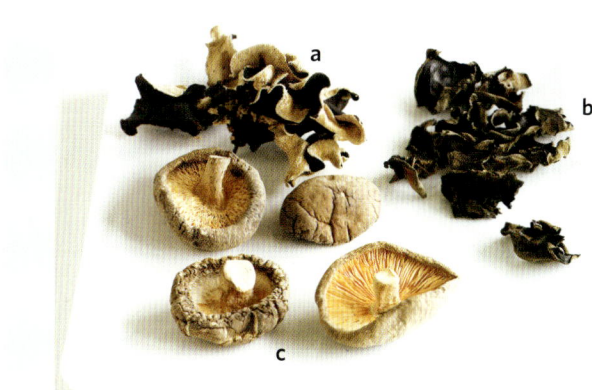

7

Chocolate Unless you're tempering chocolate, all you need to do to melt chocolate is to whack a small saucepan on the stove, heat it on a low heat for 5 minutes, turn the heat off and then break small chocolate pieces into it. Let it sit for 1–3 minutes. The chocolate will still hold its shape but shiny spots will appear. Lift it off the stove and stir vigorously with a stainless steel spoon or spatula to distribute the residual heat and melt all the chocolate pieces. Don't use a wooden spoon, as any moisture trapped in the wood will not agree with the chocolate and might seize it (that is, it turns stiff, grainy and dull).

Cinnamon (32b) comes from the brown bark of the cinnamon tree. It is widely used all over the world in both sweet and savoury dishes. It is found in either stick or powdered form. If a recipe prescribes cassia, try instead to use cinnamon, which is very similar but has a far superior flavour.

Dried woodear fungus (7a) and **cloudear fungus (7b)** both called **black fungus** and also known as woodear mushrooms.

The woodear is an edible jelly fungus, black-brown in colour, used mainly in Asian cooking. Sold dried, they need to be soaked in cool water before used. They are largely flavourless and prized mostly for their crunchy texture and medicinal properties.

Cloves (32a) are historically and predominantly used in Indian cooking. This strongly flavoured spice is best used sparingly and can be found in both whole and powdered form.

Coriander is a fragrant, citrusy, leafy green herb with a delightful fresh flavour, used extensively in Indian, Chinese and south Asian cooking, as well as in Mexican dishes like guacamole. It also can be found dried, and in seed form (which is the fruit of the plant) either whole or ground.

Cumin (32i) is a plant from the parsley family. Its seeds have a distinctive smoky, nutty flavour which are used extensively as a spice in many different cuisines, including Indian, Middle Eastern, Chinese and North African.

8

10

9

11

Durian (8) is revered in Southeast Asia as the 'king of fruits'. The durian is distinctive for its large size (up to 30cm), odour and thorn-covered, greeny-brown husk. It has large seeds and creamy yellow flesh that is very sweet when ripe. Notorious for its very pungent aroma, durian is definitely an acquired taste. Its unpleasant smell has led to the fruit's banishment from some hotels and public transport in Southeast Asia.

Eschallot (9a) is a member of the onion family but is smaller and sweeter than the average onion, and its shape appears more like a garlic clove though larger. Sometimes referred to as shallots, they, like onions, come in red and brown forms, and they vary in size.

Fermented black beans (10) are made from soy beans that have been dried and fermented with salt. These beans often have other spices, such as chillies, wine and sometimes ginger, added. They make a frequent appearance in Cantonese cooking, especially stir-fries.

Fish cakes (11) referred to in this book can be found pre-packed either fresh or frozen, in a variety of different shapes and sizes, from Chinese grocers.

Galangal (12b) is a fragrant, tough, woody rhizome with culinary and medicinal uses that originally came from Indonesia, Thailand, Malaysia, Vietnam and China. It is used in various Southeast Asian cuisines and although related to and resembling ginger, there is little similarity in taste and texture.

Gapi (4b) is a Thai fermented shrimp paste that has a pinky-purple hue and tends to be more moist and pliable than the Malaysian-Indonesian version called belachan. It can be used raw or slightly roasted.

Garlic chives (5b) are also called Chinese chives. These green shoots have a garlic flavour and are common in Asian cooking. In Chinese cuisine, they are commonly used as an ingredient in dumplings, or as part of a stir-fry.

12

14

13

15

Garlic shoots (5a) are sometimes referred to as 'garlic scapes'. These are the green shoots or tops of garlic bulbs. With a very subtle garlic flavour and a texture similar to asparagus, they are relatively new to Australia but are widely grown in many parts of Asia.

Gelatine (13) comes in powder and very thin sheets. The sheets come in many strengths but gold and titanium are the most common. The gelatine sheets are simpler and much better to use than the powder.

Ghee (14) is clarified butter made by simmering unsalted butter to remove all the moisture. The milk solids settle to the bottom and the fat is skimmed to make ghee. As a result, ghee keeps very well unrefrigerated and tolerates very high temperatures. Ghee is ubiquitous in Indian cooking.

Ginger (12c) is one of the most commonly used rhizomes in the world. It lends its flavour, peeled and sliced, to many savoury and sweet dishes throughout Asia and to many sweet dishes in the West. Originally cultivated in South Asia, it spread to East Africa and the Caribbean, and is now an integral ingredient in those regions. Other members of the ginger plant family include turmeric, cardamom, and galangal.

Glutinous rice (15a) is a white, high-gluten rice used frequently in Southeast Asian cuisine but mostly in sweet dishes. It is usually steamed with coconut milk, and when cooked takes on a sticky, dense consistency which has a 'bite' or slightly chewy texture.

Glutinous rice flour (15b) is a flour ground from glutinous rice. It is often used in dumpling skins, noodles and as a thickening agent.

Hung yoghurt (16) is a natural unsweetened yoghurt that is hung in muslin over a bowl for a few hours or overnight. As a result, all the whey drains away leaving the concentrated curd behind.

Kangkung (17) is also known as water convolvulus, water or hollow spinach and water morning glory. This semi-aquatic, leafy green is commonly grown in East and Southeast Asia and used extensively in Malay and Chinese cuisine, especially in rural areas and kampungs (villages).

Kanom jin noodles are a Thai rice vermicelli.

Kashmiri (18) is a red chilli powder which is mild but has a vibrant red colour. Made from large red chillies used in Indian cuisine, it is synonymous with tandoori meat dishes.

Keora or **kewra water (19)** is a very astringent and fragrant water that is extracted from the male flower of the *Pandanus odoratissimus* plant from east India. The water is used to flavour meats, sweets and drinks in India and Southeast Asia. This species of pandan is different to the pandan that is used for its fragrant leaves in many Southeast Asian desserts.

Lap cheong (20) is a sweet preserved Chinese sausage that is available from Chinese grocers.

Long dried chillies (21) (long skinny type) should be soaked in hot water before using. Dried chillies impart a smoky, more rounded warmth, rather than the aggressive heat that fresh chillies tend to have.

Lemongrass (12d) is widely used in many cuisines of Southeast Asia. It has a strong citrus flavor and can be dried and powdered, or used fresh. When fresh, the drier outer leaves and the green parts are usually discarded and only the pale part is used.

Mackerel (salted) (22) is found either bottled in oil or vacuum packed in Asian grocers. This salted, preserved fish has a pungent aroma which dissipates on cooking. Sometimes fried before adding to dishes, it's a great way to season dishes with interesting depth, in place of your more common Asian condiments like soy or salt.

20

22

21

23

Muscovado sugar (23b) is a minimally refined cane sugar, prized for its high molasses quotient, moisture, coarse grain and flavour. Muscovado ranges in colour from light golden to a deep brown.

Orzata (24) is an Italian bitter-sweet almond cordial, the flavour of marzipan, made from crushed apricot kernels.

Palm sugar (23d) is widely used through Southeast Asia. It is extracted from the sap of palm trees. A variety of trees are used, and the resulting sugars all vary in colour and flavour, from the pale Thai kind **(23a)** to the darker type produced in Indonesia and Malaysia. The Thais use palm sugar for savoury dishes and desserts, while the darker palm sugar is used primarily for desserts.

Pandan paste (25) is sometimes labelled 'pandan aroma pasta', which simply translates to pandan paste in Indonesian. This deep green syrup is derived from the pandanus leaf (see below)

and is used as a fair substitute for pandan leaf but it is only suitable for sweets.

Pandanus leaf (25) is used both in handicrafts and cooking in Southeast Asia. They add a distinct, beautiful fragrance, which can be described as grassy and jasmine-like, to rice, curry dishes and desserts. Fresh leaves are typically torn into strips, tied in a knot and their flavour infused into rice or liquids. Bottled pandan paste is a fair substitute but it is only suitable for sweets (see above).

Pepper (32e) is often used in Asian cooking in its white form.

Ras el hanout is a blend of Moroccan spices. There is no set combination of spices, but it can include as many as 50.

Red bean paste (azuki paste) (26) is made from azuki beans and is a sweet, maroon coloured paste originating from China. It is used mainly in a sweet context in Chinese, Japanese and

24

26

25

27

Korean cuisine, and is prepared by boiling azuki beans in water and sweetened with sugar or honey. Red bean paste can be bought in cans or plastic packets from Asian grocers.

Red fermented bean curd (27c) is used as a condiment in East Asian cuisine. This fermented tofu is made from soy beans and preserved with salt, rice wine and sesame oil or vinegar. It is sold in cubes in jars full of brine and is available from Asian grocers.

Saffron (32g) is the world's most expensive spice. It is derived from the stigmas of a particular crocus flower and provides a lovely golden yellow dye for food and fabrics. It is particularly suited to seafood and is an essential ingredient in paella and bouillabaisse.

Sesame seeds (black and white) (28) add crunch and an intense nutty flavour to food and are a popular ingredient in many cultures. The seeds come in a variety of colours, from creamy white to charcoal black with the white seeds more common in the West and Middle East and the black more valued in Asia.

Shaoxing rice wine (27b) is a traditional fermented Chinese rice wine originally produced in the Shaoxing region of China since dynastic times. It is used for drinking and is indispensable in Chinese cookery.

Shitake dried mushrooms (7c) are very popular in Chinese, Vietnamese, Japanese, Korean and Malaysian cuisine. These dark-skinned mushrooms are robust in flavour and have a substantial, meaty texture. When fresh their flavor and texture are more subtle.

Dried shrimps (29) have been dried out and slightly fermented in the sun and are used for their strong fishy flavor. They come in many varieties and sizes. Popular all over Southeast Asia, they appear in soups, stir-fries and salads.

28

30

29

31

Spring onions (9b and c) are also known as scallions or green onions. These long green edible plants with pale bulbs at the end are used throughout the world, raw and cooked.

Star anise (32h) is a dark brown, flower-like spice which adds a delicate aniseed flavour to both savoury and sweet food. It is widely used in Indian, Malay, Indonesian, Chinese and Vietnamese cooking and is one of the spices of the famous 5-spice powder used in Chinese cooking.

Taro (30) is used frequently in Hakka cuisine. It is a large root vegetable also cultivated for its edible leaves. Its flesh is pale lilac-grey, it has high starch content and an earthy flavour. It's available from Asian grocers either fresh or frozen.

Tamarind (1) or assam is a fruit used frequently in Southeast Asian cuisine in the form of dried slices, a reconstituted pulp or ready-made paste. It is used mainly in stir-fries and curries and prized for its tart, fruity characteristics.

Toban jiang (27a) or chilli bean paste is made from fermented soy beans with chilli and soy. A very salty condiment, it is used sparingly and appears frequently in Chinese cooking, mainly as a marinade or in stir-fries

Turmeric (12a and e) is a vibrant yellow coloured spice derived from the rhizome of a plant from the ginger family. Fresh or grounded, it appears extensively in Indian, South Asian and Middle Eastern cooking. Used for its bitter sweet, earthy characteristics as well as its colour, it is often employed to colour rice for special occasions.

Vanilla (31) is the second most expensive spice after saffron. It is used sparingly and derived from an orchid native to Mexico. Vanilla imparts a mellow, rich flavour and fragrance to desserts and is available in beans, extract and paste.

Yellow rock sugar (23c) is a pale yellow sugar in crystal form which imparts a wonderful, honey-like flavour to Chinese dishes.

234

32

EQUIPMENT

I'm not sure about you but when I started cooking, not knowing my kitchen equipment resulted in a few culinary misadventures, so I'll quickly outline the job each one does.

Angel food cake tin (4) is a ring tin especially made for chiffon cakes. It has a removable bottom and straight (non-fluted) sides and a flat bottom. It is NEVER non-stick.

Bamboo steamer (10)

Blender and stick blender (2 and 3) A blender is really only good for pureeing relatively soft, already broken down food, for example cooked veggies or meat, and raw fruit. Usually some amount of liquid in the mixture is required for the blades to move effectively. A regular blender will also crush ice. A stick blender is very useful for pureeing directly in a vessel, for instance when you are making soup in a pot and, with the correct attachment, it is also suitable for whipping cream.

Electric cake mixer (11) – hand held or with a stand – has very effectively replaced the elbow grease involved in whisking to aerate ingredients such as butter, eggs or cream.

Electric spice grinder is essentially a coffee grinder but it is only used for dry spices, roasted and unroasted. You're not supposed to wash the grinder, so it becomes strongly infused with spices. This being the case, it's not the most versatile piece of kitchen equipment to own. You would probably save money using a mortar and pestle instead, and, surprisingly, it doesn't take much more time.

Food processor (7) chops differently from a blender. It is capable of finely chopping (not pureeing) ingredients that don't have a high water content, like meat and nuts, very evenly, but it can be problematic when you are dealing with small quantities as the ingredients tend to get blasted to places where the blade doesn't reach, and hence it's not able to achieve an even or fine chop. It's also fantastic for making pastry quickly.

Mini food processor (8) solves the problem of chopping small amounts and is able to break down fibrous ingredients like galangal, lemongrass and dried chillies.

Mortar and pestle (12) is very useful for making pastes, like rempahs, pestos, chilli, but it's also great for crushing dry ingredients like nuts or biscuits, but do beware of strong flavours from your aromatics getting embedded in the granite and transferring onto ingredients for sweet dishes. A 20cm diameter, Asian made, granite one is the best. Anything much bigger can get difficult to handle, and the ingredients tend to creep up the sides rather than staying in the middle where you are pounding. I'd avoid anything with a smooth texture, as they don't achieve much except that they are easier to clean.

Mouli (5) is a hand cranked device used for pureeing soft fruit or cooked vegetables. It's often used for potatoes to make gnocchi.

Potato ricer (6) essentially looks like a giant garlic press and is used instead of mashing. I use it for potatoes, taro and bananas, but anything soft and starchy will pass through it.

Whisk (9) is an indispensable tool to have in the kitchen, not just for aerating ingredients but a great mixing tool, especially for removing lumps from batters.

Wok and trivet (1)

index

The ABC 'Wave' device is a trademark of the Australian Broadcasting Corporation and is used under licence by HarperCollinsPublishers Australia.

First published in Australia in 2010
by HarperCollinsPublishers Australia Pty Limited
ABN 36 009 913 517
harpercollins.com.au

Copyright © Poh Ling Yeow 2010

The right of Poh Ling Yeow to be identified as the author of this work has been asserted by her in accordance with the Copyright Amendment (Moral Rights) Act 2000.

HarperCollinsPublishers

25 Ryde Road, Pymble, Sydney, NSW 2073, Australia
31 View Road, Glenfield, Auckland 0627, New Zealand
A 53, Sector 57, NOIDA, UP, India
77–85 Fulham Palace Road, London W6 8JB, United Kingdom
2 Bloor Street East, 20th floor, Toronto, Ontario M4W 1A8, Canada
10 East 53rd Street, New York NY 10022, USA

National Library of Australia Cataloguing-in-Publication data:
  Ling Yeow, Poh.
  Poh's kitchen / Poh Ling Yeow.
  ISBN: 978 0 7333 2830 5 (pbk.)
  Includes index.
  Cookery--Australia.
  Australian Broadcasting Corporation.
641.5994

Front cover photograph by Ryan Pike
Cover and internal design by Jane Waterhouse, HarperCollins
  Design Studio
Colour reproduction by Graphic Print Group, Adelaide
Printed and bound in China by Phoenix Offset on 128gsm matt art

5 4 3 2 1   10 11 12 13 14

Prop stylist: Carlu Seaver
Food preparation: Wendy Quisumbing, Grace Campbell,
  Nick Banbury

PROP SUPPLIERS
Accoutrement
Bison
Burnt Orange
Chee soon & Fitzgerald
Dust
Japan City
Major & Tom
Malcolm Greenwood
Mud Australia
Pigott's Store
Ruby Star Traders
Sam Robinson
Signature Prints
Spotlight
Swell Textiles
The Antique General Store
Whitehouse Flowers

PHOTOGRAPHIC CREDITS
Steve Brown: pages 32, 37, 39, 41, 42, 46, 62, 87, 89, 90, 94, 101, 120 (bowl of curry), 147, 149, 151, 160, 164, 165, 173, 174, 177, 182, 208, 226-235.
Ben Dearnley: pages 14, 18, 21, 23, 26, 45, 53, 54, 59, 61, 69, 71, 73, 75, 79, 82, 92, 99, 103, 106, 113, 119, 120, 126, 130, 134, 139, 152, 157, 158, 171, 178, 184, 187, 189, 193, 194, 197, 198, 203, 206, 207, 211, 213, 214, 219, 221, 222, 225.
Jane Grove: page 29
Anthony Hill: pages 67 (top), 77, 181.
Ryan Pike: pages 30, 31, 66, 67 (bottom), 76, 108, 109, 116, 117, 124, 125.
Stephen Wong: pages 140-143.
Poh Ling Yeow: pages 17, 57, 84, 97, 133, 137, 181.